COLD
MOUNTAIN

COLD MOUNTAIN

Screenplay by

Anthony Minghella

based on the novel by

Charles Frazier

faber and faber

First published in the United States in 2003
by Miramax Books, Hyperion, ABC, Inc.
A Division of The Walt Disney Company
77 West 66th Street
New York, NY 10023

First published in the United Kingdom in 2003
by Faber and Faber Limited
3 Queen Square London WC1N 3AU

Printed in England by Mackays

Anthony Minghella is hereby identified as author of this
work in accordance with Section 77 of the Copyright,
Designs and Patents Act 1988

A CIP record for this book
is available from the British Library

ISBN 0–571–22276–5

10   9   8   7   6   5   4   3   2   1

To my family

FORWARD

Film directors have too many people to thank at the end of a project. The list of cast and crew included in this volume should contain an individual note of gratitude to each and every one of them. Directors take an authorial credit, and if it is true that, ultimately, a movie reflects the decisions and vision of one person, the director is entirely dependent on the collective contribution of several hundred people. This movie, so complex in its demands on the whole team, so full of privations that matched the hardships endured by the story's characters—months of vile weather, difficult locations, attritional working conditions—drew deep on the commitment of my established collaborators and even deeper perhaps on those working with me for the first time. If I single out some individuals here, it should not be at the expense of the whole company. It's been a battle full of heroes, even if we do not know, at the time of writing, whether the war has been won.

In any case, I am increasingly convinced that the process matters more, finally, than the result. I have lived the making of the film for more than three years; it's impossible to inhabit the progress of the movie once it is in release. In the cutting room a big brass letter B is pinned to the wall to remind me and the film's editor, Walter Murch, that we should work as hard as we can, and with rigour. B can be achieved by effort. A is only ever in the gift of an audience.

Sydney Pollack, my mentor and partner at Mirage, has again tested my compass at each stage in the process. He has lent me his experience and his wisdom with customary modesty and grace except when a producer's goad has been required, and then he has goaded, from a filmmaker's perspective, with a fellow director's respect and empathy. Bill Horberg, producing a film for me for the second time, has never wavered in his support or painstaking analysis of both creative and production matters. Albert Berger and Ron Yerxa brought the novel to Mirage and have continued to offer indefatigable enthusiasm to me throughout the making of *Cold Mountain*, while remaining guardians of a book they both loved. Tim Bricknell has been an enormous ally in the making of *Cold Mountain* from even before I began work on the screenplay. He researched with me, made many discoveries, read and challenged my illegible early manuscripts, then set out with me on the marathon journey of casting, scouting, preproduction, filming and postproduction without once losing faith or focus.

Filming the body of the movie in Romania was full of blessings, not least because it is such an untrammelled and breathtaking landscape and one that provided a glimpse of a pre-industrialised world, a landscape free of the encumbrances that prevent the deep creation of the past. What the country lacked, accordingly, was a functioning film-making infrastructure. Iain Smith had to create a production method while in production and he did so with a stern hand but great good humour and was a real friend to me. My kitchen cabinet of John Seale, Dianne Dreyer, Ann Roth, Ivan Sharrock, Mo Flam and their various teams were, again, constant and magnificent film-makers beside me as were new colleagues Paul Engelen and Ivana Primorac. Steve Andrews, my invaluable Assistant Director, got me out of trouble every day, as he has done, miraculously, on four films in a row. Derin Seale came to work as Second Unit Director in the Battle Sequence and demonstrated the flair and technical virtuosity that promises an important career making his own films. In a movie in which a fight or an animal or both lurked to test my resolve in practically every scene, Steve Dent, stunt co-ordinator, and Gill Raddings, animal-handler, made light of the tremendous burden of human mayhem and animal mayhem respectively, ensuring that neither species was damaged in the process. And Dante Ferretti, the production designer of my dreams, created location after location in partnership with Francesca Lo Schiavo: towns; farms; forests; houses—a perfectly invisible achievement -and was that director's fantasy—a collaborator without the word no in his vocabulary.

T Bone Burnett appeared amongst this group as an antic spirit, bringing his brilliant band of musicians, his uncanny ear and his deep knowledge of early American music. The songs and singers he produced perfectly complemented the work of the composer, Gabriel Yared, who gives to me the music I hear in my head, growing the film's sound picture with me, straining for perfection.

Walter Murch, with whom I have the most intimate and intense of all the film relationships, serves as editor, mixer, guide and accomplice and profoundly impacts the shape and metabolism of the movie. I am, as always, utterly in his debt.

The same debt is due to all those who appear in front of the camera. I was able to assemble, thanks to the perseverance of Ronna Kress and David Rubin, an astonishing cast and not one of them gave less than their best, ignoring sometimes appalling conditions, often freezing or baking, deprived of any creature comforts. They were a marvel, led by the indomitable Jude Law, fellow-traveller, revelation in every sense, uncomplaining in the face of being buried, submerged in a foul swamp, dragged, beaten, engulfed in a seething pit. Whatever the movie required of him, he never complained, never required me to explain. Renée and Nicole also submitted, with a certain amount of glee, to their own austerities and I remember having to stop filming one bitter morning when it was pointed out to me that Nicole was shuddering with the cold and turning blue. There was a tremendous spirit and the three of them were magnificent. Nicole has been beside me from the early stages of preproduction, passionately involved, wise, an ardent protector of the movie rather than of her own performance. Her great and true spirit presides over the film.

I must record my gratitude to the many people whose land we trampled, from North Carolina to Transylvania, and to those closer to home on whom I have sometimes trampled—not least Cassius Matthias and all my Mirage colleagues at Old Chapel Studios in London.

Finally, I thank Charles Frazier for allowing me to mess with his beautiful book. Never, even in the dark defeating days all projects must endure, did I lose sight of the privilege of working from a novel in which there was nothing to fix, just the thousand tiny diamonds Inman speaks of, and which I plundered.

ANTHONY MINGHELLA
Sunday, October 5, 2003

INTRODUCTION TO THE SCREENPLAY

I am standing inside a water-powered grist mill. The creek running beneath the mill is just audible, a faint white noise. In the scene being filmed, Ada and Ruby are supposed to dance while Stobrod, Pangle, and Georgia sing an old-time Appalachian song, "Christmas Time Will Soon Be Over." Sally Swanger, pale and mute from witnessing the violent deaths of all her family, dances too. Then the women sit and listen as the musicians perform "Wayfaring Stranger." There have already been what seem a great number of takes. Cameras are moved, lights reset. More takes. This has been going on for most of the day. It is four in the afternoon and already getting dark.

Outside all is mud, old grey patches of snow along the creek banks, low clouds. Inside, the lighting is yellow and red and warm, embodying all the features of firelight, but the room is very cold. Except for the actors, everyone is dressed in down and fleece and high-tech long underwear, and we're shivering. Plumes of vapor rise from our mouths as we breathe and speak. I'm standing jammed into a corner with a group of people, many of whom have actual responsibilities. And then there are a few like me, just watching.

I have been in any number of Appalachian mills—remnants, some of them, from the century before last. Nearly all of the ones still in operation do so as tourist attractions. They'll sell you a bag of stone ground corn meal for approximately the per-pound rate of sushi-grade tuna. But the mill I used as my model when constructing the one in *Cold Mountain* was a real working operation. As a boy of eight or nine, I used to ride my bike there after school. I was drawn to the smooth unbroken surface of dark water flowing down the race, its mossy smell, and then the white fragmentation as it fell into the pockets of the millwheel. Inside, I liked the smell of old wood and corn dust. I particularly liked the craft of the place, its lore, the work that happened there, the simple gigantic machinery that converted moving water into the turning of wheel and shafts and gears—and finally, the rolling of two huge disks of pale stone against each other to accomplish the humble job of crushing shell corn into corn meal. The whole structure vibrated with the force of an ancient technology. Even that was too much for nineteenth-century Cherokee traditionalists, inhabitants of that corner of the Southern mountains before me, who thought the use of such violence against the very stuff of life was a horrible insult to the spirit of corn. But I am not in the Appalachians. I am in Romania. The Carpathians, for God's sake. This mill is one of Dante Ferretti's subtle and wonderful creations, and it is startlingly accurate, right down to the smell of dust and water, the cobwebs in the corners. The machinery even works.

Anthony Minghella once again says, "Action." Music plays and actors act. The camera is on rails, and when it makes the turn at the corner we all draw back as the long arm that counterbalances its weight swings inches from our heads. There are stickers on the arm to commemorate the number of people it has hit. Eventually Anthony says, "Cut."

He turns to me and says, "Charles, I'm not asking a rhetorical question. This scene is in the book, isn't it?"

I say, "I'm not sure. I'd have to check."

To the best of my knowledge, neither of us is entirely joking.

Between book and movie, one or the other of us has been working with these characters, this story, for over a decade. So a certain amount of forgetting is understandable. I take it as a good thing that we are both happily uncertain at this moment about the scene's provenance. I know there is a mill in the book and that another scene has firelight and music. I don't believe anyone dances, and though "Wayfaring Stranger" occupies a significant place in the book, "Christmas Time Will Soon Be Over" is not a song I've ever heard before. In the winter of 1998, Anthony said to me that when I saw the screenplay, I'd find my rooms with other furniture in them. Or was it the other way around? In either case, I think this scene must embody his point.

I don't know what the ideal relationship between a novel and its movie adaptation is. Total adherence to the original does not always—or even frequently—make a good movie; there are many cases where faithfulness to the book leads to a lifeless movie that seems like a Cliff Notes summary. I've always thought that books are books and movies are movies. They should not be identical, nor can they be. The two forms differ too wildly in the ways they tell stories–and in fact, even in the kinds of stories they are able to tell—ever to fully correspond.

Movies desire compression—a sort of agreed-upon shorthand of narrative and character development. They have a strong affinity for linear time. They breathe easiest when they're moving straight ahead, generally at a high rate of speed. They're happiest seizing us for two vivid and exciting hours that unfold at their pace, not ours; then they send us out into the night. (Or—since I prefer matinees—throw us blinking and disoriented into the light of day.) When they work—when the right story, the right actors, the right camera work and costumes and sets all intersect—they take our breaths away.

Even the very earliest motion pictures understood the power in the compelling immediacy inherent in the technology. In one of my favorites among those pioneering efforts, an Edison short from 1896, a woman stands in a brightly lit, cluttered farmyard casting chicken feed on the ground to a mottled flock. She wears a long, dark dress and a white apron, and she goes about her work with a practiced and efficient sweep of wrist and hand. Behind her a black horse stands swishing flies with its tail. It appears to be in harness, suggesting imminent work. There is a barn and, farther back, a house. Beside the woman, a small girl mimics her distinct casting motion. The girl's grey dress and face are so near the tonal value of the poultry-yard dirt that she seems threatened with becoming invisible. Pale doves fly in and land among the chickens to eat some of the feed. They fly away. The End. The movie lasts for less than a minute. There are no cuts, and the camera does not move. And yet so much of the woman's life is given in that one laconic take. As a cinematic narrative set in a fully realized world, it is entirely satisfactory. Novels, on the other hand, are by nature expansive, baggy. They make the increasingly rash assumption that you have much more than two hours to give over to them. They love digression, the wayward. They like to loop through time, slow down, rush ahead. Then double back. They want to drag all forward momentum to a stop and tell us what the woman feeding the chickens is thinking, feeling. They desperately need to relate in great detail some tangential episode from her childhood. And then to digress for a moment about the various breeds of chickens represented in the flock. In comparison even to the simplest of movies, books are ancient technology. And what they have to offer in place of the vivid cinematic experience are the simple and slow delights of language, the increasingly archaic pleasure of following a path of words, line by line, on a journey extending across days or perhaps weeks until the experience can come to define a time in your life.

Still, if novel and film adaptation can never be twins, it seems to me that they ought to share significant amounts of DNA beyond just a correspondence of character names and the barest elements of plot, always the least interesting parts of a movie or a novel for me. The elements of Anthony's scene in the mill—the place, the characters, the sensibility—are not mine; they are his. But they are close enough relations to seem familiar to me, known. And this scene is representative of Anthony's method throughout. Related but separated elements of narrative and character development in the book undergo a convergence and concentration in the movie. Mill, music and firelight are drawn together. Two scenes of violence in the novel are merged earlier into the one horror that leaves Sally Swanger mute. Ada's gift to Ruby of her bracelet is pulled in from yet another scene in the novel. The dialogue the actors speak is not anywhere in the book. Music changes. Characters take on different colorations. Sally Swanger, for example, becomes much more of a foster-mother for Ada and Ruby than she does in my novel. Ruby is more comic. Stobrod is a generally sweeter character than I have him, part of a general adjustment in the direction of light and warmth. In the book, Ruby's acceptance of Stobrod as father is entirely an act of generosity on her part; in the movie, for her not to accept him would seem cruel. But still, they're close relations.

Part of adaptation is finding the story in the novel that a movie is able to tell. Another part is revision. When a novelist sells work to the movies, he or she is turning years of work—plot, characters, place, language, everything—over to someone else to rewrite. It is either interesting or horrifying to see what is considered changeable in the thing you've spent so much time and thought in constructing. I read a magazine article a few years ago that described a class for aspiring screenplay writers. As I recall, the instructor asks the question, "What does the screenwriter owe to the novelist?" The correct answer, shouted out gleefully by the students, is "Nothing." Of course that's mainly a glib bit of classroom showmanship; I've been a teacher and I know it when I see it. But the question still interests me. If the operative word is "novelist" rather than "novel," I have to agree with the class. The novelist is not the issue. But the original work—if it is worth taking on in the first place—is owed something. Not perfect fidelity. Not excessive respect. But it is owed a degree of commitment not to violate its essence, its heart. Otherwise, go make up your own story.

What I've known from my first conversation with Anthony in 1997 is that such a commitment is at the core of his work as a writer and director. During the long journey from book to screenplay to finished movie, there have been many, many voices in his ear, mine among them, all offering opinions. That is a troubling thought for a novelist, since ours is not a collaborative process, but Anthony very serenely invites this participation, and so must find it occasionally helpful. I'm also sure that he must sometimes wish we would all shut up and let him make his movie. Of these numerous and sometimes disparate voices, I particularly thank him for listening foremost to the story, the characters.

CHARLES FRAZIER
October 2003

COLD
MOUNTAIN

1. INT. TUNNEL. PREDAWN. JULY 1864.

Shadows and shapes. A BARREL rumbles along the tunnel. It reaches a kneeling figure, who rolls it forward. A relay team. At the end of the tunnel, where it widens, a man, naked to the waist, crouches, stacking the barrels.

> UNION SOLDIER
>
> I can hear them. Can you hear them? Rebs right over our heads.

> UNION SOLDIER 2
>
> Shh! If we can hear them, they can hear us.

> UNION SOLDIER
>
> Enough powder here to blow a hole in the sky.

> UNION SOLDIER 2
>
> A real Yankee Good Morning.

2. EXT. CONFEDERATE LINES. PREDAWN. JULY 30, 1864.

A STAND OF TREES. FIRST LIGHT. Peace and beauty. A RABBIT surfaces from its hole, shakes itself from the ground, darts into open ground to confront the FORBIDDING TRENCHES OF THE UNION AND CONFEDERATE ARMIES, RANGED AGAINST EACH OTHER ON THE OUTSKIRTS OF PETERSBURG. Wooden barricades in the shape of crosses define the two lines. The Federals have been laying siege for weeks. So early and it's already too hot. The trees are an oasis of green in a world of mud between the two stark and ugly scars of the trenches.

A LOW CHANT BEGINS, THE CHEROKEE LANGUAGE, SWIMMER'S VOICE.

CAPTION: PETERSBURG, VIRGINIA. JULY 30TH, 1864. IN THE FOURTH YEAR OF THE CIVIL WAR.

3. EXT. BEHIND CONFEDERATE LINES. PREDAWN. JULY 1864.

OAKLEY—a raw, teenage soldier—his wheelbarrow filled with salvaged uniforms, weaves away from a pile of freshly filled coffins, negotiating the complex of trenches.

4. EXT. 25TH NORTH CAROLINA TRENCH. PREDAWN.
JULY 1864.

Men are rousing, boiling water for coffee or to shave, smoking, stiff from the night. Another RABBIT is disturbed from its hole, ears pricked up to a distant rumbling. Some soldiers are picking over the uniforms in Oakley's wheelbarrow.

INMAN, a severe figure, gaunt and bearded, opens his book—a battered leather volume. THERE'S A TINTYPE IMAGE OF A YOUNG, GRAVELY BEAUTIFUL WOMAN.

He examines a new jacket and its ominous bullet hole. His own uniform is hanging off him. He peels off the jacket, tears off the patch with his name on it. SWIMMER is already sewing, as he translates:

> ### SWIMMER
> *—Your spirit will wane and dwindle to blue, the color of despair—*
> *this is your path. There is no other.*

> ### INMAN
> *And that's supposed to work?*

You have to say it in Cherokee.

INMAN

You said it to me in Cherokee.

He begins sewing INMAN into his jacket.

5. INT. TUNNEL. PREDAWN. JULY 1864.

The CROUCHING MAN has wrapped FUSE WIRE around the last barrel and now retreats, paying out the wire as he does so, as each man in the tunnel crawls backward behind him.

6. EXT. CONFEDERATE LINES. PREDAWN. JULY 1864.

Oakley, freshly recruited, nervous of snipers, keeps his head low.

ROURKE

Don't worry, son. Those Yankee boys keep store hours. They ain't open yet.

7. EXT. UNION LINES. DAWN. JULY 1864.

The CROUCHING MAN emerges from the tunnel. He's covered in sweat, half naked, and desperate for air. Men go past him, carrying sandbags into the tunnel to block up its mouth. The fuse wires, plaited from three into one, are lit. Then he climbs up to consider the Confederate lines.

8. EXT. CONFEDERATE LINES. DAWN. JULY 1864.

A RABBIT darts along the lip of the trench. Butcher sees it, beckons to another Cold Mountain boy, Rourke.

> BUTCHER
>
> That's fresh breakfast. *Shoot him!*

> ROURKE
>
> *I'm not firing, start the damn war back off.*

Butcher chases after the rabbit, Rourke in raucous support.

> BUTCHER
>
> That's my rabbit!

Great sport as he wrestles with Rourke. Inman, fifty yards away, looks over, amused, as Rourke takes the lead.

9. INT. TUNNEL. DAWN. JULY 1864.

The fuse fizzes back toward the barrels. The frame fills with smoke and an incandescent bluish light.

10. EXT. CONFEDERATE LINES. DAWN. JULY 1864.

ROURKE is still running after the rabbit, BUT NOW THE GROUND BUCKLES UNDER HIM AND HE'S BEING LIFTED SLOWLY INTO THE AIR, the earth swelling as a small hill appears, causing cannon and men to slide down this sudden slope.

AN APOCALYPTIC EXPLOSION. FOUR TONS OF DYNAMITE RIP THE GROUND OPEN IN A CRATER 135 FEET LONG, 90 FEET ACROSS, 30 FEET DEEP. FLAMES AND SMOKE MUSHROOM UP, HORSES, GUNS, MEN ARE BLOWN TO PIECES AND THROWN UP INTO THE AIR. INMAN IS SUCKED BACK ALONG THE TRENCH UNTIL THE WORLD SEEMS TO FALL ON TOP OF HIM.

HE DISAPPEARS UNDER DIRT AND DEBRIS. A STRANGE
MUSIC PLAYS.

11. EXT. BLUE RIDGE MOUNTAINS, NORTH CAROLINA. DAY.
SPRING 1861.

FROM THE SHROUD OF BLUE MIST, MOUNTAINS SLOWLY
EMERGE: like a Chinese watercolor, undulating into a smudged horizon.
Below them, a CABRIOLET races along a verdant track. The driver is a
man in his early fifties, dressed in the severe garb of a minister. MON-
ROE. And next to him, elegant in the elaborate, architectural skirts of the
period, is his daughter, ADA, the face in Inman's tintype.

12. EXT. CHAPEL, COLD MOUNTAIN TOWN. DAY.
SPRING 1861.

A WOODEN JOIST swings across the view of the Blue Ridge.
Construction workers, including Butcher and Rourke and Oakley, swarm
over the roof of an unfinished CHAPEL, below which appears the small
town of COLD MOUNTAIN. Swimmer is running up a thin trestle
toward the roof section and then along its skeleton, fearless, carrying a
long plank over to INMAN, who works, knees gripping a rafter, hammer
in hand. They're all three years and a whole lifetime younger.

The cabriolet swings down into town, almost absurdly elegant for the
rough and ready nature of Cold Mountain. Swimmer skips over to Inman,
cuffs him to get his attention. Inman looks down as the cabriolet halts
and Ada steps out, an angel in a wild place. UP ON THE ROOFBEAMS
OF THE CHAPEL, the men are preoccupied with talk of secession from
the Union.

                              ROURKE
        (hammering)
        I call this nail Northern Aggression.

BUTCHER

(hammering)

I call this nail a free nigger.

Monroe greets the workers. He's their new minister. Esco Swanger, a town elder and glorious curmudgeon, comes down to meet him.

MONROE

Mr. Swanger, good morning to you.

ESCO

Esco.

MONROE

Esco, and you remember Ada . . .

ESCO

Miss Monroe.

ADA

Good morning.

MONROE

(to the others)

Good morning. *Noah would have been delighted to have built his ark in Cold Mountain.* In Charleston, my congregation would still be disputing the size of the windows.

ESCO

It's a chapel. Four sides and a roof.

MONROE

(going to the plans)

Exactly. Now you recall I want the benches facing in.

To the side of the chapel, women are setting up a lunch for the workers. Ada joins them. She has the circumspect air of the bluestocking, uncomfortably aware of the dirt beneath her hem and the men's radar for her every move. Inman watches as Esco's wife, SALLY, approaches her.

> SALLY
>
> Miss Monroe, I was just thinking about you. Cold Mountain must feel like the end of the world.

> ADA
>
> Not at all. It's very beautiful.

> SALLY
>
> Well, you put us all to shame. Men up here had a bearing on what they thought a woman was—and then you showed up.

> ADA
>
> I doubt that.

> SALLY
>
> Oh, believe me—if you would just say a word to one of these fools, I could get my top field cleared.

> ADA
>
> Any one? *Like a forfeit?*

> SALLY
>
> *(pointing at Inman, who immediately looks away)*
> No. Him in particular, up in the rafters. Been pressing me since the day you arrived here.

> ADA
>
> Your top field cleared?

Ada comes over, carrying a tray of cider glasses. Calls up to Inman.

> ADA (CONT.)
>
> Good morning.

Inman swings down. He feels the other men staring, burning a hole in his head.

                              ADA (CONT.)
I'm Ada Monroe.

                              INMAN
Inman.

                              ADA
Inman?

                              INMAN
W. P. Inman.

                              ADA
W. P. Inman.

                              INMAN
Repeating a thing doesn't improve it.
(shrugs)
People call me Inman.

                              ADA
If you were to take a glass of cider your friends might stop staring. Inman.

                              INMAN
They're not my friends.

He drops down to ground level, takes the cider, scowls at the other guys. They're breaking for lunch and—as they make their way to the trestle tables—they enjoy jostling Inman.

                          INMAN (CONT.)
Thank you.

ADA

And what do you do?

INMAN

I work wood. Hunt. Mostly work wood.

ADA

Clear fields?

INMAN

(*uncomfortable*)
I can clear a field.

ADA

So, was there something in particular you wished to say to me?

INMAN

(*thinks about it*)
Not that comes to me.
(*hands back the glass*)
I'll say thank you for the cider.

And he heads over to join the other men gathering around the tables for lunch. Ada watches him, intrigued. Rourke and co. approach ESCO, who has no truck with a war he judges to be based on a conflict between one type of wealth and another.

ROURKE

Esco loves the Yankees.

ESCO

I prefer a Yankee to a halfwit.

Inman arrives just as Rourke points a warning finger at Esco. He pushes the finger down to get by. Esco continues:

ESCO *(cont.)*

What is it you think you'd be fighting for?

ROURKE

The South.

ESCO

Last time I checked, south was a direction.

Esco's sons, ELLIS and ACTON, who're working at the other end of the building, have now arrived at the table.

ACTON

Pop, you causing trouble?

ESCO

No.

ELLIS

That means yes.

ESCO

You cut the wood, you carry the water for good old King Cotton. Now you want to fight for him. Somebody has to explain it to me.

ACTON

(to Butcher and the others)
Don't even try.

The others are desperate to tease Inman.

ROURKE

How's the cider? Sweet?

Ada, at the cider stand again, watches them laughing at Inman, who keeps his head fixed on the table as Monroe begins to say grace.

13. EXT. SWANGER FARM. COLD MOUNTAIN. DAY.
SPRING 1861

A PIANO, lashed to a cart, bounces along the lane, passing the Swanger
Farm where Esco, Acton, and Ellis are working in the surrounding fields.

Sally comes out to look. It's Ada riding next to one of the farm-hands, a
second boy keeping watch over the piano. Sally goes over.

                    SALLY

That's a fine-sounding thing.

                    ADA

My piano. I've been missing it.

                    SALLY

Thank you, by the way.
(from Ada's quizzical look)
Inman's over in the top field, clearing his debt.

                    ADA

Oh dear. And then he had nothing to say.

                    SALLY

He was happy.

                    ADA

Really?

                    SALLY

Are men so different in Charleston?

                    ADA

Men? I don't know. In Charleston I was called a thistle, twice,
by two different men. Both of them—they were hunting for a
simile—thistle came right to them.

If you're saying you might like him, why not go over and say good morning.

14. EXT. BOTTOM FIELD, SWANGER FARM. DAY. SPRING 1861.

Inman's in the field, stripped to his undershirt, hot work, WORKING A PLOW, THE HORSE'S REINS WRAPPED AROUND HIM. He hears something and looks up. At the edge of the lane, ADA TURNS TO PLAY A FEW NOTES ON THE PIANO, which is still strapped to the cart. Then she briefly raises a hand to Inman, who smiles, waves back, watching as the cart rumbles off down the track.

15. EXT. BATTLEFIELD. POST EXPLOSION. DAY. JULY 1864.

PAGES OF INMAN'S BOOK, THE TINTYPE OF ADA, FLUTTER AROUND.

OAKLEY, his clothes ripped from him, walks by, finding himself wandering on a new planet. Or dreaming. There is smoke instead of air and the ground, empty of what was before, is now strewn with unidentifiable stuff, coated with clay, some of it moving. He wanders on this moonscape, having lost all sense of direction. A HORSE, its limbs spastic and failing, struggles to its feet. Oakley watches its faltering run into the wall of smoke, which seems itself to be dancing, until he realizes he is watching shoals of gleaming FEDERALS, pouring across no-man's-land, roaring the roar of attack.

The FEDERALS, yelling their attack, flood toward the crater, hundreds of them, charging towards the enemy, charging into the wall of dense and impenetrable smoke.

Around Oakley, stunned and bewildered Confederates try to make sense of what has happened. Some of them see the Federal charge and run. Others, some naked from the explosion's blast, pick up their rifles. Oakley watches the enemy's charge, closer and closer until they, too, become part of his dream. THEY SEEM TO DISAPPEAR INTO THE GROUND.

THE FEDERALS HAVE FUNNELED DOWN INTO THE GREAT GASH OF THE CRATER. THEY POUR IN, AND THEY CAN'T GET OUT AGAIN, arriving at an insurmountable wall of mud. THEY ARE CRUSHED AGAINST THIS NEW BARRIER, THE REAR PRESSING INTO THE FRONT, UNABLE TO UNDERSTAND THE NEW TOPOGRAPHY.

The Confederates regroup. Orders are yelled. Chaos is developing into battle. Some of them, understanding their advantage, begin firing down into the crater.

In the rubble, there is movement, as Inman struggles out of his temporary tomb, coughing out dirt. He sees the ruined book, the battered tintype, retrieves what he can. Then he stumbles forward to where he sees Rebels firing. He arrives at the lip of the crater, passing Swimmer, who has also survived, and is wandering, stunned.

BUTCHER

It's a turkey shoot.

INMAN

What?

BUTCHER

A turkey shoot. They've run themselves into a hole. Hell's busted.

What Inman sees below him is a terrible carnage. The Federals caught in a death trap. Mortar, pushed to the edge, is firing up into the air, the shells going up and then almost straight down into the crater, exploding over the heads of the helpless enemy. Some cannon have been pushed into the trenches that route into the crater. Each ball causes terrible damage. The Confederates have made a pincer movement outside the crater, forcing all the Federals in. It's medieval. No escape.

Inman sees the dead and the living standing side by side, a monochrome clay color from the smoke and debris and crushed against each other, unable to properly fight, unable to fall. Confederate soldiers next to him are firing, then receiving a freshly loaded rifle, then firing again. Swimmer joins in, collecting discarded rifles and throwing them, bayonets fixed, like spears.

In the pit, somebody waves a handkerchief of surrender. And a Confederate looks down sympathetically and there's a respite. He leans in, his ankles held, and is able to pull up the surrendering Federal, who has clambered up the steep side of his hellhole. Others follow. Inman and Swimmer help, too, pulling up the defeated Federals. Then somebody is helping out a soldier only for A TRACE OF BLACK SKIN TO APPEAR UNDER THE FILM OF GRAY. There's a moment of surprise and then the Confederate releases the surrendering hand in disgust—there is no love lost between the Confederates and Black Federal soldiers. Shooting breaks out again, hard to say which side starts first, but then there is a vicious return to the fray. Someone shoots the Confederate who had initiated the rescuing.

CONFEDERATE REINFORCEMENTS ARRIVE and jump into the pit to engage the Federals in hand-to-hand fighting, swarming into the crater. Inman goes in with them. Too close for rifles, just bayonets and guns swung like clubs, and now Inman is sliding down into that hell, Bowie knife flashing. Primitive. Unutterable carnage. Men killing each other in embraces, soldier crushed against soldier, desperate to survive, to kill, to live. An oozing layer cake of bodies, dead and frantically alive, drowning in slick.

YOUNG OAKLEY is near Inman. He loses his rifle and picks up A CARTRIDGE CASE, clubbing his opponent, then slips onto him and is stuck with a bayonet, the pain of which makes him squeal.

Inman goes at it. He's a warrior, punching and stabbing. A coldly efficient killer. He's grabbed from behind and crushed, a hand gouging at his face, an almighty struggle. He falls back against Oakley, and he and his Federal opponent fight to the death with the wounded boy as their pillow. It's like fighting in a swimming pool; bodies separate the opponents, they can barely reach each other across the dead and dying. The slaughter continues over and around them, the sound, the sound of hell and madness. Oakley has his arm around Inman, like lovers.

16. EXT. THE BATTLEFIELD. DAY. JULY 1864.

FIGHTING OVER: Some orderlies pass, lifting OAKLEY away on a blanket. Oakley's pale as a maiden, the life leaking from him. Inman walks a way with him. Oakley looks up, desperate to be brave.

                    OAKLEY
     I got a few. You saw?

                    INMAN
     I saw.

                    OAKLEY
     Am I going to die?

Inman flicks his eyes to the orderly, whose look confirms the boy's wounds are certainly mortal.

Inman sits, the boy's blood all over him. In the mud, still in the grip of a buried hand, he sees A HUGE REVOLVER, A LEMAT. He retrieves the gun, examines it, nine rounds and then a short shotgun barrel. The crater, below him, an abattoir of men. The victors are yelling, pumped mad with adrenaline. Butcher yells up at him from the crater.

                    BUTCHER
     *That was something! That's hell and we've been there! We've seen the
     elephant!*

A WOUNDED BLACK SOLDIER sits up as Butcher celebrates. Butcher runs over but can't find a charge for his musket. He looks around in the stack of corpses, pulling out weapons, tries one: it's not loaded, he throws it down, tries another: not loaded. The wounded man can't get up, tries to drag himself like a crab away from Butcher. Inman yells at him, appalled.

> ### BUTCHER(cont.)
> You got a charge?

He picks up another musket. It fires. The wounded Federal falls back, dead.

17. EXT. CONFEDERATE LINES. DUSK. JULY 1864.

THE AFTERMATH. The dead being piled up for burial, divided into allegiance. Wounded prisoners able to walk are led away. A great deal of casual looting—of boots, of equipment, of personal items. Inman sees a Rebel, extravagantly costumed, a strange FIDDLE head protruding from his knapsack.

This is STOBROD THEWES. He's bent over a dead Federal, examining his mouth. He reaches behind his back and roots around in the knapsack, producing A PAIR OF PLIERS, WHICH HE INSERTS INTO THE CORPSE'S MOUTH. He's yanking away when A SWINGING BOOT connects with his ribs and knocks him to the ground. Startled, he looks up to see Inman hovering over him.

> ### STOBROD
> That's gold in his mouth he got no need for.
> *(shrugs)*
> We take his boots.

He examines his fiddle for damage.

18. INT. FIELD HOSPITAL. NIGHT. JULY 1864.

Inman sits on the ground beside Oakley's cot. Around them, the wounded and dying, makeshift care, lanterns, groans.

OAKLEY

I'd like to hear some music before I go.

19. EXT. CONFEDERATE LINES. NIGHT. JULY 1864.

Inman walks around the campfires. He hears some fiddle music. It's Stobrod. He heads toward the music, with purpose.

20. INT. FIELD HOSPITAL. NIGHT. JULY 1864.

Stobrod stands over Oakley. Consults with Inman.

STOBROD

What about "Bonaparte's Retreat"?
(scratching a few bars)
That's one I play.

OAKLEY

Play me something sweet. Like a girl's waiting for me.

Stobrod looks at Inman, confused.

OAKLEY (CONT.)

Play me something like there's nothing to fear from a merciful Lord.

INMAN

(to Stobrod)
You heard him.

STOBROD

(nervous)
I only know a couple of tunes.

OAKLEY

Like when you're thirsty up at Bishop's Creek and the water is
so cool.

Inman glares at Stobrod, who feels cornered.

STOBROD

I don't know what music that is.

But he starts to play, hesitant, then with gathering confidence, improvising, increasingly expansive, as if he's as surprised as everyone else.
Oakley's lips move. A whisper. Inman leans in.

OAKLEY

I'm reaching Cold Mountain before you.

Stobrod plays. It's wrenching. Oakley stills. Inman abruptly puts his hand
on the neck of the fiddle, stopping Stobrod. The boy is dead. Inman gets
to his feet and walks away.

21. EXT. BLACK COVE FARM. NIGHT. SPRING 1861.

It's pouring with rain. INSIDE THE FARMHOUSE, ADA IS PLAYING
THE PIANO AND SINGING. Men and women crowd into the parlor,
in best clothes, celebrating the completion of the chapel. Inman arrives,
stands outside on the porch, his coat soaked, water pouring off his hat. He
looks at Ada. She finishes. Monroe steps in front of the applause, smiling.

MONROE

Friends, my daughter and I are very happy to have this opportunity to thank you, from our hearts, all of you, for your kind
welcome and, most of all, for a fine Chapel. It's a good thing to
pray in a place made with your own hands. So, thank you and
bless you. This house is always open, to any of you, at any
time. I pray that God grants me many days to return your
generous welcome to us both.

His words of thanks leak through the window to Inman, who watches, listening, willing Ada to notice him. And then she does.

22. INT. PARLOR, BLACK COVE FARM. NIGHT. SPRING 1861.

Monroe goes over to Ada. He nods at a group of men who congregate in one part, not mingling. Their leader, TEAGUE, might be a minister himself, favoring a black dress coat, a black crow in the corner, eyes flashing. Beside him is Bosie, young, beautiful, sinister, almost albino, a strangely elongated fingernail. And stunted twins, Mo and Jo. Ada doesn't know them. Esco comes over.

> MONROE
>
> Esco, our friends there—
> *(indicating Teague and co.)*
> —they helped build the chapel?

> ESCO
>
> That's Teague and his boys. One time the Teague family owned the whole of Cold Mountain. My farm, your farm, all belonged to his grandpappy. Teague wanted this place bad. You got it. He's here sniffing out an advantage.

> MONROE
>
> There's no advantage here, but to celebrate a job well done. Cheers—
> *(he raises his glass)*
> —and thank you.

And Teague raises his glass across the room.

23. EXT. BLACK COVE FARM. NIGHT. SPRING 1861.

Ada appears at the door, opening it onto the porch. She's carrying a tray with drinks. Acknowledges Inman.

ADA

Were you never planning to come inside?

INMAN

I'm wetter than a fish.

ADA

There's a good fire going.

INMAN

I'm all right. You're always carrying a tray.

ADA

I'm taking some root beer over to the Negroes. Somebody said
you were enlisting. Are you?

INMAN

If there's a war, we'll all fight.

ADA

(*unimpressed*)
If there's a mountain we'll all climb, if there's an ocean we'll
all drown.

INMAN

I don't much care for a man from Washington telling me how
to live.

ADA

Better it be a man from Charleston.

INMAN

Or a woman from Charleston.

ADA

Did you get a picture made?

INMAN

Say again.

ADA

A tintype, with your musket and your courage on display.

INMAN

You're laughing at me.

ADA

I don't know you.

Now Teague appears. On his way somewhere, but he slows, waits, deliberately invading their space. Then his cohorts appear, Bosie and the twins, Mo and Jo. They all glance over at Inman and Ada. Then they head off into the night. As Teague goes:

TEAGUE

Hoo-Hoo! Said the barn owl.

Ada and Inman watch the gang go, turn back to each other. They're awkward.

INMAN

This doesn't come out right. If it were enough just to stand. Without the words.

ADA

It is. It is.

INMAN

You look at the sky now, what color is it? Or the way a hawk flies. Or you wake up and your ribs are bruised thinking so hard on somebody. What do you call that? Better just to stand.

(immediately takes the tray)

I'll do that. I can't get much wetter.

He goes into the night rain. She watches him.

24. EXT. CONFEDERATE TRENCHES, "HOTEL." NIGHT.
JULY 1864.

Men grabbing sleep in makeshift sleeping quarters dug out of the clay
walls of the trenches. Inman is repairing his book by the sickly candle
lantern next to his bedroll, salvaging the pages, attempting to straighten
the bent tintype of Ada. An OFFICER comes along the trench,
approaches Inman, who makes to stand.

                    OFFICER
        Don't get up, soldier. You are mentioned tonight in my
        report. You men from Cold Mountain have once again been
        heroes to the cause.

                    INMAN
        (tight)
        Sir.

                    OFFICER
        I know. A bloody day. It's what our general said, son: Good thing
        war is so terrible, else a man might end up liking it too much.

                    INMAN
        Sir.

                    OFFICER
        (has a mission for Inman)
        There's a dozen Yankees in that stand of trees between us.
        Stuck there from the retreat. Tomorrow morning they can
        shoot us down for sport.

He turns away. Inman rubs his face. Shakes Swimmer awake.

25. EXT. EDGE OF CONFEDERATE LINES. NIGHT. JULY 1864.

A beautiful night. Lots of stars. Inman and three others, including Swimmer and Butcher, slide over the top of the trench, far to one side of the stand of trees. The plan is to cast a wide arc that will bring them around back of the trees, closer to the enemy side than their own. The four men crawl over the ground. They pause. Inman has arrived at a tangle of corpses. He slithers over them.

They work their way toward the trees. THERE ARE A HALF-DOZEN FEDERALS CROUCHING IN THE COVER OF THE TREES. They are dozing. Only one of them sits with a rifle surveying the Confederate lines, the others have their backs to the enemy, sitting against the trunks, grabbing a few minutes' sleep.

As the four Rebels approach, still crawling, one of the Federals opens his eyes, sees the attack, shifts for his rifle. INMAN STANDS UP, FIRING INSTANTLY, killing him and two others, while Swimmer throws himself at another. The exchanges are brief and savage, and Butcher is hit and all of the Federals lie dead. Inman goes to Butcher, but there's nothing to be done. Then the Rebels break from the trees.

A FLARE goes up, then another, both from the Federal trenches. INMAN AND HIS ACCOMPLICES ARE PICKED OUT IN A BRILLIANT GREEN LIGHT. Shots follow, from both sides, aimed at the three returning men as they zigzag toward their own lines. As they get close, voices cry out, rippling down the trench, joining their own admonitions: Don't shoot, Hold your fire, they're our boys, Hold your fire!!! They're almost home. Swimmer is laughing, whooping. Then just as suddenly he falls, wounded. Inman stops, turns back, runs to him.

Inman collects Swimmer, drags him, carries him. They're twenty yards from their lines. A BULLET CATCHES INMAN IN THE NECK. He goes down like a tree, blood pouring from his neck. Lying on the ground, he watches the phosphorescent lights slowly fade to black, all sound fading with them, REPLACED BY A SOUND OF BEATING WINGS, ANXIOUS, PERCUSSIVE.

26. INT. CHAPEL, COLD MOUNTAIN TOWN. DAY.
SPRING 1861.

A BIRD IS CAUGHT INSIDE THE NEWLY COMPLETED CHAPEL.
It flies in short, terrified bursts, hitting windows. Ada is there, then
Inman enters. Gradually she and Inman close in on the bird; Inman
removing his coat to use as a net.

27. EXT. CHAPEL, COLD MOUNTAIN TOWN. DAY.
SPRING 1861.

Ada emerges, then Inman. They're like unwitting newlyweds. THE
WHOLE TOWN IS THERE, WAITING TO CHRISTEN THE NEW
CHAPEL. Inman releases the bird into the air. Monroe invites his congre-
gation inside the chapel, greeting each member, as does Ada. Music,
"Lining Out," sung by the entire church, begins as she shakes Inman's
hand and he goes inside.

28. EXT. BLACK COVE FARM. DAY. SPRING 1861.

A beautiful day, the farm peaceful. Inman walks up the path to the farmhouse, its borders flowering and pretty, a slave woman weeding. He
knocks on the door. Monroe answers.

MONROE

Mr. Inman.

INMAN

Reverend.

MONROE

What can I do for you?

Inman hovers, awkward. Ada appears, awkward.

INMAN

I have some sheet music. Belonged to my father. No use to me.

Ada comes forward, takes the package.

MONROE

You must come in.

INMAN

I should probably get along.

ADA

Mr. Inman is more comfortable outdoors. Perhaps we might take a walk.

MONROE

A splendid idea.

29. EXT. BLACK COVE FARM. DAY. SPRING 1861.

Monroe and Inman and Ada touring the farm. It is well-tended by the dozen slave farmhands who work it, some of whom are dotted about in the landscape. Rolling mountains dominate the view.

MONROE

I want to get sheep into this field. A big field doesn't look right without sheep. You're a lucky fellow, Mr. Inman, you've had this view all your life.

INMAN

I think so.

MONROE

It's a special view. I dragged my poor daughter to Cold Mountain from Charleston because of my doctors—they say my heart is weak—so the air's supposed to do me good. But it's the view I think heals.

(*turns to Inman*)

I have no plans to preach war in my church, Mr. Inman.

INMAN

I imagine God is weary of being called down on both sides of an argument.

MONROE

I imagine he is.

Monroe is intrigued by Inman's response. Ada walking behind, comes alongside the two men, threading her arm into her father's but, by so doing, also arriving next to Inman.

30. INT. PARLOR, BLACK COVE FARM. DAY. SPRING 1861.

From the window Ada watches the Cabriolet head toward town, Inman sitting next to Monroe.

At the piano, Ada unwraps the leather lace from the package of music. Inside the first book of music, there's a tintype of INMAN, a typical Confederate pose. Some of the music has left its imprint on the picture, the notes like a melody over Inman's face. Ada picks them out on the piano and then that fragile phrase is drowned by the ebullient sound of Shape Singing. A noisy choir letting rip—

31. INT. CHAPEL, COLD MOUNTAIN TOWN. DAY.
MAY 20, 1861.

—THE WHOLE CHURCH IS SINGING FROM THE SACRED HARP BOOK, ARMS FLAGGING THE RHYTHM. Inman is there, as is Ada. He fixes on her neck, the way her hair falls.

The door bursts open. Young OAKLEY, apologetic nod to Monroe, sits at the back, then leans forward, as the singing continues, to say something to Rourke, who says something to Butcher, the news spreading like wildfire. Rourke gets up, leaves. Butcher gets up next, follows. Another man. Another. Depleting the male voices, until only women and some of the older men are singing and one side of the church is practically empty. Inman remains, fixed on Ada, who looks around at him.

32. EXT. CHAPEL, COLD MOUNTAIN TOWN. DAY.
MAY 20, 1861.

Those left in the congregation now spill out into what has become a melee as the NEWS OF SECESSION goes up.

Enormous excitement, particularly among the boys, who now seem curiously attractive to the girls. Inman blinks out into the sun, Ada finds him. They're awkward as they watch other sweethearts embracing.

ADA

Well, you have your war.

TEAGUE AND HIS MEN COME RIDING UP THE STREET, their horses clearing a path among the celebrating crowd. Teague reins in his horse and rides it up against Esco Swanger.

TEAGUE

Those who follow Lincoln, or preach abolition, best keep one eye open when they're sleeping, Old Boogie Man might get you!

Inman steps between Esco and Teague, holding the reins of Teague's horse, easy and dangerous. Bosie watches.

INMAN

Are you the law all of a sudden?

Teague produces a document, which he waves in the air.

TEAGUE

That's right, son. Home Guard for Haywood County. I'm the law from today. You all go fight now. We'll watch your sweet-hearts.

He rides away, *stopping at the cart from Black Cove, where two of Monroe's slaves wait.*

TEAGUE (cont.)

And guard against the Negro. They want what the white man got. Give them the chance, they'll carry rape and murder to your firesides.

MONROE

The only slaves within twenty miles labor on my farm. Which you know, Mr. Teague.

BOSIE

Captain Teague.

MONROE

They're good Christians and I'll vouch for them.

Inman walks to Ada.

INMAN

You might be safer back in Charleston.

ADA

But then who'll be waiting for you?

They both want to get to the point of declaration but don't know how. They stand, people noisy around them, those about to leave, those about to be left.

33. EXT. BARN BEHIND CONFEDERATE LINES, PETERSBURG.
DAY. SUMMER 1864.

Inman, with several other wounded men, is stretchered out of the Barn for
rail transportation to a hospital. The urgency of the siege continues. An
ORDERLY PASSES HIM AND INMAN GRABS AT HIM. THE
ORDERLY BENDS TO LISTEN.

                         ORDERLY

   What book?
   (more whispering)
   I'll look, soldier, but you know—

Inman clutches him. Another croak, Inman barely conscious.

                    ORDERLY (CONT.)

   I said I'd look.

The orderly stands up, a good man. He glances at one of the stretcher
bearers, who shakes his head: a needle in a haystack.

34. INT. BEDROOM. ROOMING HOUSE. COLD MOUNTAIN
TOWN. DAY. SPRING 1861.

INMAN SITS ON HIS BED, wearing pants and a vest. His room is like a
monk's cell. Nothing in it. Inman's trunk is packed. He's polishing his
boots, in his bare feet. One hand inside the boot, the other blacking it.
There's a knock at the door. He opens it. It's Ada. He abruptly closes the
door on her.

35. INT. HALLWAY, ROOMING HOUSE. COLD MOUNTAIN
TOWN. DAY. SPRING 1861.

Ada waits outside. She's not sure what's happening. Then Inman opens
the door. He's buttoning his shirt. His boots are on, one conspicuously

dirty, one highly polished. Somebody walks up the stairs, carrying a jug and bowl. They separate as the man passes them. They're tender, awkward.

                                    ADA

I found you this book. William Bartram. They tell me it's good. I think he writes about these parts, the author, so . . .

Inman takes it. She has something else. Wrapped in paper.

                              ADA (CONT.)

And this . . .
(hands it to him)
I'm not smiling in it. I don't know how to do that, hold a smile, so now I'm solemn.

                                  INMAN

Ada . . .

                                    ADA

What?

HE KISSES HER, pressing into her, his arm circling her waist. Below them the sound of a MARCHING BAND. It's the RECRUITMENT PARADE and brings Rourke and Butcher racing down the stairs. Inman pulls away from Ada as the boys hurtle for the front door.

                                  ROURKE

Let's go!

36. EXT. COLD MOUNTAIN TOWN. DAY. SPRING 1861.

Rourke, Butcher, and then Inman appear in the doorway of the rooming house, and then fall in with the motley crew of volunteers AS THEY MARCH BY WITH THE BAND AND THE ENLISTED SOLDIERS.

The town is out to wish them well—parents, younger brothers, sweethearts walking alongside their brave men. Ada looks down from the balcony of the rooming house. Inman looks back and sees her, but almost immediately loses her in the crowd. THE DRUMMERS DRUM, THE CROWD CHEERS, THE RECRUITS MARCH UP THE HILL—

37. EXT. BEHIND CONFEDERATE LINES, PETERSBURG. DAY. SUMMER 1864.

THE TRAIN TO TRANSPORT THE SERIOUSLY WOUNDED BEGINS ITS JOURNEY AWAY FROM THE CONFEDERATE LINES. As it slowly gathers momentum, belching steam, the ORDERLY catches up to it, clutching the Bartram. Jumps on the boxcar.

38. INT. BOXCAR. DAY. SUMMER 1864.

A CROWDED WAGON. It's a cauldron, and those able smash through the wooden walls to make a breathing hole. Some have their heads thrust out like crated poultry. INMAN IS IN THERE, an ugly seepage from his bandaged neck. THE ORDERLY FINDS HIM, PRESSES THE BOOK INTO HIS HANDS. Inman nods his thanks, and the orderly disappears. *The light plays black and white through the boarded sides of the boxcar, flashing on Inman's face as he drifts in and out of consciousness. A FIDDLE PLAYS, THEN A BANJO.*

Inman focuses and sees the strange head of STOBROD'S FIDDLE. Stobrod is serenading him, accompanied by an angel-faced and extremely heavy child-man, PANGLE, whose grin of delight seems permanent even in this claustrophobic, grim world. Inman is panicked, putting a hand out to push the fiddle away. His voice is a croak, spoiled.

INMAN

I'm not dying.

STOBROD

(to Pangle)
What'd he say?

PANGLE

Says he ain't about to die.

STOBROD

(to Inman)
Truth to tell, they say you are, soldier. We'll meet again, in the better world.

He changes his tune, and the tempo, finding a foot-slapping rhythm, the two musicians grinning at each other. Inman lapses back into unconsciousness.

39. INT. HOSPITAL, CHARLESTON. DAY. SUMMER 1864.

INMAN lies, bandaged, eyes closed, in THE BALLROOM OF A COLONIAL MANSION, co-opted as one ward of a Confederate hospital. Rows of beds, the wounded and the dying, are lodged between some vestiges of the room's former glory. SOME LOCAL WOMEN, conscious of their duty to the cause, are brought through by an exhausted doctor, who's lost all his grace. The windows are open, but it's still insufferably hot, the muslin curtains barely moving.

DOCTOR

Most of these men will be dead by the morning or, if they're stubborn, by nightfall. I have other men outside in the quadrangle waiting for the beds.

The women try to process this, the attitude.

DOCTOR (CONT.)

So, any kind word will be a blessing.

One woman is overpowered by the stench, and gags.

> DOCTOR (CONT.)
> It's the heat. I'm sorry. They rot.

The women begin to approach the beds.

> DOCTOR (CONT.)
> Don't pray. If they're not God-fearing, you can stir up a
> hornet's nest. This isn't a meeting of the good ladies of
> Charleston.

MRS. MORGAN, nervous, decent, sits next to INMAN. His mouth is
moving. She doesn't know what he's saying.

> MRS. MORGAN
> I'm sorry, you want water?

She bends to him again. His voice is a faint croak.

> INMAN
> Pigeon River. Little East Fork.

The doctor is on his exit, stops at the bed.

> MRS. MORGAN
> I'm sorry. I don't know what he's saying.

> DOCTOR
> They ramble. Names of loved ones.

> MRS. MORGAN
> (listening to Inman)
> Pigeon River. Is that a place? Cold Mountain?

The doctor shrugs, not a detective, and moves on, stops at the man in the
next bed. Has a brief look, calls to a nurse.

DOCTOR

This man is dead.

40. EXT. APPROACH TO BLACK COVE FARM. DAY.
AUTUMN 1863.

Cold Mountain at its loveliest. The CABRIOLET with Monroe and Ada
heads toward Black Cove. At a bend they meet Teague, Bosie, and the
others, riding furiously toward them. Monroe reins in the trap and lets
them thunder past before continuing on their way home. Monroe keeps
glancing at Ada.

ADA

What?

MONROE

You're looking—at this moment, I don't know why—you're
looking exactly like your mother.
(they ride in silence)
Do you worry when there's no word from him?
(no response)
From Mr. Inman?

ADA

Yes. But then I've tried counting the number of words which
passed between Mr. Inman and me.

MONROE

I lost your mother after twenty-two months of marriage.
Things enough to fill a lifetime.

ADA

Every time you see the doctor you get melancholy.

MONROE

He listens to my heart and I get emotional.

34

He gives you alcohol and you get emotional.

She squeezes his arm.

MONROE

We commiserate about the folly of this terrible war.
(looking ahead, seeing smoke)
Is that a bonfire? So close to the house.

Then they see THE FAMILY OF SLAVES *turn off the road as their cabriolet approaches, running away into the fields.*

MONROE *(cont.)*

(shouting at the disappearing slaves)
Hey! Stop there! Hey!

THE BARN IN WHICH THE SLAVE FAMILY HAD LIVED IS ON FIRE.

A FIGURE SWINGS IN THE HEAT OF THE FLAMES, HANGING FROM A BEAM. *Monroe spies it as they drive up the lane.*

MONROE *(cont.)*

Dear God.

ADA

No, Daddy, it's not real.

The figure swings round. IT'S AN EFFIGY, A GROTESQUE CARICATURE OF A BLACK MAN. *Monroe dismounts the trap.*

MONROE

(appalled)
What is wrong with us all?

41. EXT. BLACK COVE FARM. LATE AFTERNOON.
AUTUMN 1863.

Monroe and Ada are outside, a picnic at the summer table, autumn leaves blowing up around them. Nearby the charred skeleton of the barn. Ada gets up, clears away. Monroe stays her for grace.

MONROE
For your Providence, oh Lord, we thank thee.

ADA
Amen. That was the last of the ham.

MONROE
It was delicious.

ADA
I have to learn how to cook.

MONROE
I was going to say something in chapel. Perhaps some of the womenfolk will volunteer.

ADA
I can't have people coming here and cooking for me!

MONROE
It's my fault. I should have raised you less like a companion and more like a young woman. I'm sorry, Ada. And for dragging you here.

ADA
I'm not sorry, and you know I would have followed you any-where—to Mongolia! But with no one left to work this place and nothing to buy, nothing to buy it with, I just don't know how we'll get through another winter. And the farm going to rack and ruin.

MONROE

Will you play me something? Something peaceful while I look over my sermon.

ADA

It's too damp out here. You should come inside. I'll bring you a blanket.

Ada takes the dishes away.

42. INT. PARLOR, BLACK COVE FARM. DUSK. AUTUMN 1863.

ADA PLAYS THE PIANO. Outside in the garden, Monroe has adjourned to his striped campaign chair and is hunched over his notes. The door of the parlor is open and the music floats over to him as he works.

Ada plays. A FEW SPOTS OF RAIN appear at the window. Then the steady drumming of a summer shower. Ada continues to play.

ADA

Daddy, bring the tablecloth in with you!

She plays some more. Monroe hasn't come in. The rain splashes onto the window.

ADA (CONT.)

Daddy, come inside before you drown!

After a few more bars, she stops playing and, curious, goes to the door. She stands at the doorway. MONROE'S SERMON IS CAUGHT IN THE WIND AND BLOWS AROUND HIM, THE INK RUN TO ABSTRACTIONS, his hand dropped and visible to Ada as, with dread, she approaches. SHE CATCHES THE SODDEN PAPERS, CHASING AFTER THEM, THEN REACHES HER DEAD FATHER. He's like a fish, his face shining with the rain, and glass-eyed. She leans in to him, her head to his heart, then runs, oblivious to the rain, her dress already drenched, runs down the lane.

43. INT. HOSPITAL, CHARLESTON. NIGHT. SUMMER 1864.

INMAN'S FACE as he drifts in and out of consciousness. Mrs. Morgan, the hospital volunteer, sits by Inman's bed. She holds ADA'S UNOPENED LETTER, badly weather-damaged, the pages stuck together, the writing blurred where the ink has run.

MRS. MORGAN

You have a letter. It's come to you by way of Virginia.

There are various dates, which she decodes.

MRS. MORGAN (CONT.)

It's not too recent—written this past winter. I'm afraid I can't read who it's from. Dear Mr. Inman,—

ADA (V.O.)

Dear Mr. Inman . . .

44. EXT. CHAPEL. DAY. LATE WINTER 1863.

Ada approaches the chapel and examines the tintypes of the dead soldiers from Cold Mountain.

ADA (V.O.)

Since you have left, time has been measured in bitter chapters of who has fallen and who will not return from this terrible war. And no word from you . . .

45. INT. HOSPITAL, CHARLESTON. NIGHT. SUMMER 1864.

Mrs. Morgan reads to Inman, trying to decipher the letter:

> ADA (V.O.)
> Are you alive? I pray to God that you are.

46. INT. ROOMING HOUSE. COLD MOUNTAIN. DAY. SPRING 1864.

Ada is outside Inman's room. She looks behind her, at the chapel, then considers the door, tries it, looks inside—the bare room, marks on the walls.

> ADA (V.O.)
> I will not leave Cold Mountain . . .

47. INT. BLACK COVE FARM. NIGHT. WINTER 1863.

Ada is writing. A lonely room. She touches her father's prayerbook. Grieving.

> ADA
> . . . but I do not know how to be who I must become to survive, hating to rely on charity from those who can least afford it . . .

48. EXT. BLACK COVE FARM. DAY. SPRING 1864.

EVERYWHERE SIGNS OF PROFOUND NEGLECT, like a Grimm's fairy tale of a deserted house. The fields are overgrown with weeds, the gardens abandoned. The chickens have deserted the henhouse and are wandering around the outbuildings, scuffing at the packed dirt. Sally and Esco approach, carrying a basket of food, some preserves. They negotiate the chickens, the creepers breaking through the porch, and knock at the door.

SALLY

Ada! Ada, it's Sally.
(to Esco)
Well, set it on the porch.

They're seen from ground level, through a boxwood, as their feet patrol the ground, turn away from the door, and then retreat, their voices drifting away. Ada is there, crouching in her hideaway, a blanket on the ground, her book. She wants to reveal herself but is too embarrassed.

ESCO

Will you look at the state of this place!

SALLY

Poor soul. She's got nobody and nothing and three hundred acres of misery.

During this, a ROOSTER struts into the boxwood. As the rooster approaches, Ada shudders, tries to shoo it away without alerting her presence. Ada peers through the boxwood as Sally and Esco close the gate and recede. The rooster comes at her again. She rises up, kicking out at it, while he flares his wings, spurs flaying at her. Ada runs from the boxwood, tormented by the triumphant rooster, which continues to fly and scratch, driving her into the house.

49. INT. ADA'S BEDROOM. BLACK COVE FARM. DAY.
SPRING 1864.

Ada dabs at the scratches, her dress rolled down to the waist to reveal her arms and shoulders, all the while dipping into the crock of Sally's preserves. Now she shucks off the dress completely and tries to find a clean replacement. There isn't one, so she hunts through the overflowing laundry basket for something less dirty.

50. INT. MONROE'S BEDROOM, BLACK COVE FARM. DAY.
SPRING 1864.

Ada, still carrying her grief, reluctantly enters her father's room, wearing
undergarments. Everything as he left it and, in contrast to the rest of the
house, extremely tidy. She opens a wardrobe, finds one of his coats, puts it
on. It's much too big, and she rolls up the sleeves, catching her pinched
face and disheveled face in a swivel mirror.

ADA (V.O.)
. . . So much time has passed. My father is dead. Black Cove
abandoned and me, left hostage to my own fears and frailties.

51. INT. HOSPITAL, CHARLESTON. NIGHT. SUMMER 1864.

MRS. MORGAN
So now I say to you, plain as I can
(can't read the next bit)
—then something I can't read,

52. EXT. BLACK COVE FARM. DAY. WINTER 1863.

A strong wind, winter. Ada bent double in the gale as she tries to coax a
cow into the barn.

ADA (V.O.)
. . . if you are fighting. Stop fighting. If you are marching,
stop marching.

53. EXT. BLACK COVE FARM. DAY. WINTER 1863.

Ada digging, trying to find potatoes. Sodden. Slips over.

This war is being lost on the battlefield and is being lost twice
over by those who stayed behind.

54. INT HOSPITAL, CHARLESTON. NIGHT. SUMMER 1864.

MRS. MORGAN

—come back to me. Come back to me is my request.

ADA (V.O.)

. . . come back to me, come back to me is my request.

Inman is very still. Then, eyes glinting with determination, gives a TINY
NOD.

55. EXT. THE OCEAN BY THE HOSPITAL, CHARLESTON. DAY.
SUMMER 1864.

THERAPY FOR WOUNDED SOLDIERS. Some of those convalescing
swim or are helped to paddle in the healing sea. There are rudimentary
wheelchairs. Inman, a long way from home, is among those sitting in one
of these, very still, gray and sick—but alive. He pulls at the dressing on
his neck, exposing the still raw and livid wound to the sea air. Inman has
his Bartram, his bookmark is the battered and foxed picture of Ada,
which he considers before continuing to read.

Behind him A HUNDRED SLAVES AT WORK IN THE FIELDS, and
behind them the mansion that has become the hospital.

A series of bells, of shouts, and the slaves stop working, prepare for the
long walk home, congregating, then forming a line, herded by the fore-
men. Inman eases his position to bend over and dip his bandage in the
seawater. He brings the wet bandage to his neck, considers the ocean, his
fellow ragtag of wounded, the slaves, the great fields, the mansion. The
whole meaning of this war around him.

56. EXT. APPROACH TO BLACK COVE FARM. DAY.
WINTER 1863.

IT'S WINTER. A solitary RIDER jogs his horse through the frost, toward Black Cove Farm.

Ada is working at a pump, failing to coax water from the well. She's wrapped in blankets. The farm is somewhat unkempt and so is she. The hem of her skirt is frayed. She rips at it, tearing off a strip of material, which she binds around the handle in an attempt to thaw the mechanism. Then she looks up to see the horseman approaching. It's Teague. Ada immediately heads inside the house.

Teague arrives at the house, takes a brace of RABBITS from his saddlebag. He heads for the gate. The gate needs oiling, the path is overgrown. He looks at the pump handle, the abandoned pitcher. Ada opens the door, pinning her hair.

> TEAGUE
>
> *It's taken me too long, but I've come to pay my respects.*

> ADA
>
> *Thank you.*

> TEAGUE
>
> *(hands over the rabbits)*
> *I reckoned you might need fattening up.*

Ada takes them. She is very queasy with these dead animals.

> TEAGUE *(cont.)*
>
> *This house must bring bad luck. Killed my grandpappy to lose it, then my daddy died on account of not having it, then your daddy died on account of getting it. We should burn it down.*

> ADA
>
> *Didn't somebody try?*

TEAGUE

Lot to manage without help. Need a hand with that pump?

ADA

No, I don't.

TEAGUE

I'm happy to volunteer.

ADA

But not to volunteer for the war?

TEAGUE

The war? I wanted to go. But you know: too old, too literate. Plus I got no spleen. Lost it from a horse's kick.

ADA

You've got no spleen.

TEAGUE

That's the thing about an organ. You don't know you need it till you lost it.
(produces a Bowie knife)
I want to clear this path. I can just as soon do it and talk as stand around and talk. Then you can say men beat a path to your door.

ADA

I'd really prefer it if you didn't do that.

TEAGUE

Would you rather I did my job?
(hacking at the path)
—see if there's any material I should confiscate. For the war effort.

ADA

I was raised in the good manners of the South, where a gentleman doesn't enter a house with a woman alone.

TEAGUE

(*now he's at the pump*)
Good manners didn't quite make it to these mountains. If it don't
yield meat, or you can't sit on it, or suck on it . . .
(*he gets the pump going, water pours out*)
And you're sleeping all right?

ADA

I'm sleeping fine.

TEAGUE

These cold dark nights?

He stands on the porch, surveying the land he believes to be rightly his, his back to
Ada. Walks slowly down the steps.

57. INT. BLACK COVE FARM. NIGHT. WINTER 1863.

Ada, starving, ransacks the desert of her kitchen. A weak oil lamp reveals THE
TWO RABBITS, partially covered on a plate, flies buzzing around them, a little
liquid leaking from them. She can't bear them there, gathers them up and runs out.

58. EXT. BLACK COVE FARM. NIGHT. WINTER 1863.

ADA BURIES THE TWO RABBITS. The wind howls. She covers the little
hole with soil and stones. Thinks she hears a noise, listens, alert to any unfamiliar
sounds, then hurries back to the house.

59. EXT. CHAPEL, COLD MOUNTAIN TOWN. DAY.
SPRING 1864.

—A tintype is added to the chapel's votives. There are fifty or more images now, the
paint flaking around them. The exterior of the chapel, three years on, has taken on

the burden of recording history. There is no minister, although Ada is there, witnessing, anxious at the news of those lost, but no services, just the votives, tintypes, or simply the names of those missing in action, accompanied by tiny vases of wildflowers. The town shrouded in mist, and quiet.

60. EXT. TREE PROMENADE, CHARLESTON. DAY. SUMMER 1864.

Inman and a number of other walking wounded make their way, under supervision, toward the town. The grandeur of the approach, the carriages. The sorry state of the soldiers.

61. INT. COURTHOUSE, CHARLESTON. DAY. SUMMER 1864.

TWO GREAT TRESTLE TABLES, LOADED WITH CLOTHES. Underneath the tables, boots—laced together, origins various. The charitable womenfolk are helping match clothes to recovering soldiers, some of whom are still on crutches or in wheelchairs. Inman finds a black dress coat, some pants, a pair of boots. He accumulates a little pile. On his way out, AN ELDERLY AND STAUNCH CONFEDERATE GENTLEMAN shakes his hand and gives him an apple from the barrel.

62. EXT. TEMPORARY BARBERSHOP, CHARLESTON. DAY. SUMMER 1864.

Inman emerges from the courthouse and looks down on the makeshift barbershop set up outside the courthouse.

Two barbers, two chairs. A blind man is selling peanuts, singing as he does so. A very elegant square, some stucco-fronted buildings, a glimpse, if distressed by the war, of the moneyed south in sharp contrast to the modest town of cold mountain. An auction house opposite advertises slaves, cattle, land. Inman passes the Blind Man.

BLIND MAN

Getting better?

INMAN

Seems that way.

BLIND MAN

I wouldn't hurry. War's almost done. Don't need your help to lose it.

INMAN

Where'd you take your wound?

BLIND MAN

Before I was born. Never saw a thing in this world, not a tree, a gun, or a woman. Put my hand on all three.

He's shoveling some peanuts into a twist of paper.

INMAN

What would you give for that? To have your eyeballs for ten minutes?

BLIND MAN

Ten minutes! Wouldn't give an Indian head cent. Might turn me hateful.

INMAN

That's sure what seeing's done to me.

BLIND MAN

That ain't the way I meant it. You said ten minutes. It's having a thing and then the loss of it I'm talking about.

INMAN

Then we don't agree. There's not much I wouldn't give for ten minutes of someplace.

BLIND MAN

Someplace or someone?

BARBER

(to Inman)
Next.

BLIND MAN

You watch yourself. They're shooting men who take themselves a walk.

Inman settles in the seat. The barber, anxious, contemplates the livid,
scabbed wound on his bearded neck.

BARBER

I'll cut your hair, but I ain't about to shave you. That thing
opens up, your head's liable to fall off.

INMAN

Let's take that chance.

63. INT. HOSPITAL, CHARLESTON. PREDAWN. SUMMER 1864.

Inman's face. It is almost dawn. The window by Inman's bed is a frame
giving onto the still dark world. The Night Guard passes by on its patrol
of the perimeter. A CLEAN-SHAVEN INMAN IS FULLY DRESSED
UNDER THE COVERS. He gets his hat, pushes his book into his knapsack, and with one step up, WALKS OUT OF THE WINDOW AND
INTO THE WORLD.

64. EXT. THE OCEAN BY THE HOSPITAL, CHARLESTON.
DAWN. SUMMER 1864.

Inman, his footprints in the sand, as he hurries along by the edge of the
ocean, away from the hospital . . .

BOSIE (O.S.)

By order of Zebulon Vance, governor of this great state of
North Carolina: any soldier turned deserter is guilty of treason
and shall be hunted down like a dog—

65. EXT. COLD MOUNTAIN TOWN. DAY. SUMMER 1864.

Ada walks down the hill, curiously dressed in her father's coat. There is an
absence of young people, but the older folk are gathered around the
General Store, where Bosie, flanked by Teague and the twins, is reading
from a state proclamation. Ada has to walk around them to enter the
store. Bosie develops a nosebleed.

BOSIE

—Any man takes in a deserter is likewise guilty of treason.
The Home Guard is powered to enter any place it sees fit,
without notice or constraint. Names of all deserters will be
posted in every town, published in every newspaper.

66. INT. GENERAL STORE, COLD MOUNTAIN TOWN. DAY.
SUMMER 1864.

The proclamation continues outside as Ada enters. Ada approaches Mrs.
Castlereagh, the owner.

ADA

Is there a letter for me?

MRS. CASTLEREAGH

Nothing—we're getting no post through at all. The sooner we
lose this war the better. They say not one boy in ten is coming
home.

ADA

May I speak with you please?

Ada walks purposely to the back, where there's a small room. Mrs. Castlereagh follows. Ada has A POCKET WATCH in her purse, which she produces. It's all hard for her, shaming:

ADA (CONT.)

This was the Reverend Monroe's. It's a special watch—you can see the mechanism, it's—I don't know who would want a watch . . . who can bear to look at the time?

MRS. CASTLEREAGH

I can let you have a little pork. Keep your daddy's watch.

ADA

Thank you.

MRS. CASTLEREAGH

I was talking to the other womenfolk about looking in on you, at Black Cove. Right now is hard, but—

ADA

I manage very well. Whatever the talk is. I'm grateful for the pork. Which I intend to pay for. Of course.

67. EXT. GENERAL STORE, COLD MOUNTAIN TOWN. DAY. SUMMER 1864.

Ada emerges and almost collides with Teague. She wriggles past him.

TEAGUE

Is everything all right?

68. INT. CHAPEL, COLD MOUNTAIN TOWN. DAY. SUMMER 1864.

Ada sits in the empty chapel eating the pork, ravenous. Teague enters, his voice disturbing her.

TEAGUE

He's not coming back. You know that. You must know that in your heart. *I can't bear to see you carrying a torch for a ghost.* I worry about you. Look at me. I'm not nothing.

There is a moment, then Ada hurries away. He watches her go.

69. EXT. SWANGER FARM. DAY. SUMMER 1864.

Ada walking home, oblivious to the beauty of the mountains behind her. She's bent, the wind kicking up around her, as she nears the Swanger place.

SALLY (V.O.)

Ada . . .

Sally Swanger calls out from the field. She's concerned at Ada's gaunt, ragged appearance. Ada waits for her approach.

SALLY (CONT.)

You're skinny as a whippet, girl—you're coming indoors with me.

ADA

I can't, I'm not—I need to clean some clothes.

SALLY

Great God, you ever looked at my husband! I can't get him to wear decent church clothes Christmas morning. *Hang on to me, the wind'll blow you over.*

And she folds her arm into Ada's. They walk up the lane.

70. INT. SWANGER FARM. AFTERNOON. SUMMER 1864.

Ada eats. Esco across from her contemplating her evident appetite, the oversized man's jacket. Sally ladles more food onto Ada's plate.

> SALLY
>
> *Don't go back to that dark house. There's a bed here, least till our boys get home.*

> ESCO
>
> That your daddy's coat?

> ADA
>
> I was saying to Sally, I wasn't expecting to be visiting, so—

> ESCO
>
> Don't suit you.

He starts to chuckle, then Ada, too, then Sally.

> ESCO
>
> I can't get up to your place this week.
> *(of Sally)*
> She's mad at me—

> ADA
>
> I don't expect—

> ESCO
>
> —more than I can do to keep this place half managed. I'm ready to stop, I tell you. I just want to sit on my porch with Sal, watch my boys in the field, holler "Good job!" every hour or so.

> SALLY
>
> That'll be a good day when our boys get home. What about your people in Charleston?

ADA

There are no people. And no money. My father had some
bonds and investments. They're worthless now, of course, the
war has . . . they're not worth anything.
(they look at each other)
I've got nowhere else to go. I don't want to go.

ESCO

And waiting on a feller.

A look from Sally.

ESCO

Look down our well.
(Sally's disgusted with him)
She should! Look down our well with a mirror, you'll see the
future. S'what they say.
(to Sally)
You do it!
(to Ada)
She does it.

SALLY

I know it ain't rightly Christian, but it's what folks do, like
when they dangle a needle over the belly to see if you're carrying a boy or a girl.

ADA

What kind of mirror?

71. EXT. YARD, SWANGER FARM. LATE DAY. SUMMER 1864.

AN IMAGE—DISTORTED, WATERY. IT'S HARD TO RESOLVE
BUT COULD BE A GORGE, THE SUN LOW, THE SILHOUETTE OF
A FIGURE WALKING SLOWLY FORWARD, A SUDDEN DISTUR-
BANCE OF CROWS.

Ada is bent backward over the well, a hand mirror glinting down into the blackness. The reflection is elusive against the bright evening sky, the sun almost set, and low.

> ESCO
>
> See anything?

> ADA
>
> I don't know.

> SALLY
>
> I tried many a time, never saw a dickey bird.

The image is clearer. The figure walking, the steep incline of the gorge's corridor, all fiercely black and white as if it were a carpet of snow and black hieroglyphs of rock, and crows flying. The trick of the glass and the watery disk of the well surface. Then the figure seems to suddenly pitch forward, but at that moment, Ada—canted over, getting dizzy—has to move and the image flies away, replaced with the sky, the flash of the setting sun.

> SALLY (CONT.)
>
> You all right?

Ada's faint. She sits up, blank, a little shaken.

> ADA (V.O.)
>
> Yesterday I found myself crouched over a well like a mad-woman, which I suppose I have become—

72. EXT. BLACK COVE FARM. LATE AFTERNOON. SUMMER 1864.

Ada is writing in her father's campaign chair, a blanket wrapped around her, a rake propped next to her.

ADA (V.O.)

—and staring down into its secrets, I thought I saw you there, walking back to me—or wished I did.

RUBY (O.S.)

Them cows wants milking.

Ada looks up from her writing with a start. She covers her letter, guiltily, instinctively. In front of her, at the gate, is A YOUNG RAWBONED, FERAL WOMAN, barefoot, and dressed in a hand-dyed shift of blue. Her name is RUBY.

RUBY (CONT.)

If that letter ain't urgent, is what I'm saying.

ADA

I don't know you.

RUBY

Old Lady Swanger says you need some help. Here I am.

Ada is instantly defensive, intimidated.

ADA

I need help, I need, I do need help, but I need a laborer—there's plowing and rough work and—I think there's been a misunderstanding.

RUBY

What's the rake for?

ADA

The rake?

RUBY

Ain't for gardening, that's for sure. Number one—you got a

horse, I can plow all day. I'm a worker. Number two—there's no man better than me cause there's no man around who ain't old or full of mischief. I know your plight.

ADA

My plight?

RUBY

Am I hard to hear, 'cause you keep repeating everything. I'm not looking for money, never cared for it and now it ain't worth nothing. I expect to board and eat at the same table. I'm not a servant. Do you get my meaning?

ADA

You're not a servant.

RUBY

People'll have to empty their own night jars, that's my point.

ADA

Right.

RUBY

And I'm not planning to work while you watch, neither.

ADA

Right.

RUBY

Is that a yes or a no?

ADA

The rake: there's a rooster—he's the devil, I'm sure of it. He's Lucifer himself. I go near him, he's at me with his spurs.

RUBY

I despise a flogging rooster. Where is he? My name's Ruby
Thewes. I know your name.

Ada gets up, nods to the corner of the yard. Ruby goes over. The rooster
gathers himself up for a new opponent. IN ONE MOVEMENT SHE
PICKS UP THE BIRD AND TWISTS OFF ITS HEAD.

RUBY (CONT.)

Let's put him in a pot.

73. EXT. MARSHLANDS. DAWN. SUMMER 1864.

AN ARMY OF TINY CRABS scuttle across the sandy marsh. A LARGE
HAND grabs at a clutch of them. Inman, starving, swills the crabs in a
puddle then proceeds to eat them. Horrid taste. Keeps chewing. Now he's
walking along the path between two islands of marshland. He moves warily, his beard longer, his figure gaunt, his clothes weathering to a uniform
smudge of charcoal.

74. EXT. PLANTATION. DAY. SUMMER 1864.

Inman walks through thick grass, passes a small lake. Great cranes fly
heavily over him. An alligator swims lazily, head breaking the green surface.

75. EXT. A BLUFF. NIGHT. SUMMER 1864.

INMAN WALKS A ROCKY TRACK, FALLING AWAY TO THE
RIVER AT ONE SIDE, A STEEP CLIFF TO THE OTHER, the way
itself broken and precarious, bad country to meet an enemy.

Inman sees A LIGHT in the distance, a torch flicking in and out of view, like a star to follow. He stops, narrows his eyes to focus on the view, listening hard. He pulls out the LeMat.

A MAN, ALL IN BLACK, A HORSE IN TOW, IS AT THE EDGE OF THE GORGE. The horse has a burden—a sack or wrapped bundle—draped over either side of the saddle. The man attempts to heave the bundle onto his shoulders. He can't, and the bundle slips to the ground, cover falling enough to glimpse an arm, a head. IT IS THE BODY OF A BLACK GIRL. The man tries again to lift her. He's clearly upset, despairing. His hat falls off to reveal dandy's long hair, all extravagant curls. He staggers with the weight of the girl, heading for the lip of the deep gorge.

> VEASEY

God forgive me for doing this. I'm so sorry. I'm sending you to a better place.

He kisses the girl again and again, cheeks, mouth, mumbling to her. He's at the edge now and can just let her go. THEN INMAN'S GUN IS AT HIS TEMPLE.

> INMAN

Don't do that. *Just back up, nice and steady, do this all in reverse, you're going to end up with her draped back over your animal.*

> VEASEY

Don't pull that trigger. I am a man of God.

> INMAN

I've killed several of them.

> VEASEY

I mean I am God's minister.

INMAN

What part of God's business is throwing a woman down a gorge?

VEASEY

A slave woman, can you see that in this light? She's black as a bucket of tar.

He's retreating, on his way back to the horse.

INMAN

Is she dead?

VEASEY

Drugged her. Like you would a butterfly. And I care for her, that's the heartbreak of it.

He has the girl back on the horse. Inman brings the torch up to his face. It's tearstained.

VEASEY (CONT.)

She's got my bastard in her belly. *What kind of pistol is that? I never saw the like of it.*

76. EXT. VEASEY'S TOWN. NIGHT. SUMMER 1864.

Inman leads the horse, with Veasey ahead of him, hands tied behind his back, desperate for a reprieve.

VEASEY

I'm begging you. It's better you blow out my brains than return me to this place.

INMAN

Where does she live?

VEASEY

She sleeps in our kitchen. You don't know me, friend, but the good Lord punished me with want. That's all I do all day: want—food, the female parts . . .

INMAN

Shut your mouth. I don't want a sermon every time I ask you a question.

They're in the town's main drag now. There's a chapel and, next to it, a small house.

INMAN *(cont.)*

This your place?

VEASEY

Dear God of misery.

INMAN

You're going to put her back where she sleeps.

VEASEY

I do that, the members will lynch me. Consorting with a nigger, adultery, siring a bastard while serving as their preacher. We're a strict congregation—we've churched men for picking up a fiddle on the Sabbath.

INMAN

So you reckoned to kill her.

Disgusted, Inman approaches the front door of the house.

VEASEY

There's a back door. Have pity.

And he leads Inman down a side path.

77. INT. VEASEY HOUSE. NIGHT. SUMMER 1864.

Veasey comes in, now carrying the girl. Inman comes behind, the gun trained on Veasey as he sets her down by the fire.

VEASEY
(*whispering*)
Thank you. I was going to do a grievous wrong.

He looks longingly at the girl as he puts the blanket around her shoulders. He turns to Inman.

VEASEY (CONT.)
You tasted dark meat? Sweet as licorice. I think I should go back up to my wife. She wakes at the slightest noise.

Inman is incredulous that he thinks he can just go to bed.

INMAN
Where's some paper and a pencil?

78. EXT. CHAPEL, VEASEY'S TOWN. DAWN. SUMMER 1864.

INMAN HAS TIED A DISTRAUGHT VEASEY TO A TREE IN FRONT OF HIS CHAPEL. Inman is pinning a sheet of paper above Veasey's head. It's covered in handwriting. A dog barks.

VEASEY
You're not entitled to judge me! You're nothing but an outlier, plain as daylight! God strike you down and—!

Inman has pulled a handkerchief from Veasey's jacket. He stuffs it into his mouth, cutting this diatribe short. And then he walks away, leaving Veasey tied to the tree, cursing through the handkerchief.

79. INT. ADA'S BEDROOM, BLACK COVE FARM. PREDAWN. SUMMER 1864.

Ada wakes up to persistent knocking.

> RUBY (O.S.)
>
> Ada? Ada? You up?

> ADA
>
> Yes.
> *(opening her eyes)*
> It's still dark.

> RUBY (O.S.)
>
> Tell the cows that. It's late.

80. INT. KITCHEN, BLACK COVE FARM. PREDAWN. SUMMER 1864.

Ada enters blearily, clutching her novel. Ruby is already busy.

> ADA
>
> I have to eat something.

> RUBY
>
> Then you have to get up earlier.
> *(at Ada's book)*
> What's that?

> ADA
>
> A novel.

> RUBY
>
> *(heading outside)*
> You want to carry a book, carry one you can write in—

81. EXT. BLACK COVE FARM. DAWN. SUMMER 1864.

Ruby emerges, followed by Ada, chewing on a carrot.

                    RUBY
    —we got our own story. Called Black Cove Farm:
    a catastrophe.

She looks back at Ada for a reaction.

                    RUBY(CONT.)
    I can spell it, too. Learned the same place you did, in the
    schoolhouse. That's one of the first words they taught me.
    Ruby Thewes, you are a c-a-t-a-s-t-r-o-p-h-e.

They're heading for the stable.

82. INT. STABLE, BLACK COVE FARM. DAY. SUMMER 1864.

Ruby's already pitching hay. Turns to Ada, hands her a rake. Ada, half
asleep, accepts obediently, stunned by this energy.

                    RUBY
    Three years I was in school before my daddy—saying God rest
    his soul is like wishing him what he had in life, 'cause he lived
    to rest, he was born tired—before my daddy decided there was
    better use for me than have me sat all day in front of a chalk-
    board.

83. EXT. A FIELD OF WEEDS, BLACK COVE FARM. DAY.
SUMMER 1864.

Ruby dictates a list to Ada as they bustle along.

RUBY

    Number one—lay out a winter garden for cool-season crops: turnips, onions, cabbage, greens.

Ada scribbles, walks, scribbles.

84. EXT. BARN, BLACK COVE FARM. DAY. SUMMER 1864.

Ruby up a ladder, inspecting the roof.

RUBY

    Number two: patch the shingles on the barn roof. Do we have a maul and froe?

ADA

(writing, holding the ladder)
Maul?

RUBY

Maul. M-a-u-l.

ADA

I have no idea.

85. INT. SPRINGHOUSE, BLACK COVE FARM. DAY. SUMMER 1864.

Ruby cleans out leaves and detritus from the stone channel, allowing the stream to flow free and cool.

RUBY

    Number three: clay crocks for preserves. Peppers. Beans. Jams.

86. EXT. BOTTOM FIELD, BLACK COVE FARM. DUSK. SUMMER 1864.

Ruby doing her version of soil analysis, scrunching the earth, tasting it, spitting it out. Ada makes a face.

> RUBY
> Clear and turn this field. No harm done letting it go fallow, now we'll do well.

87. EXT. OUTBUILDINGS, BLACK COVE FARM. AFTERNOON. SUMMER 1864.

Ruby looks up. Ada catches up with her.

> RUBY
> Number fifteen—

> ADA
> Sixteen.

> RUBY
> Number sixteen: let's hang some gourds for a martin colony. Keep away crows. You got one thing in abundance on this farm, and that's crows. Shut the gate.

88. EXT. APPLE ORCHARD, BLACK COVE FARM. DUSK. SUMMER 1864.

Ruby, delighted, contemplates the bounty of apples.

> *RUBY*
> *There's survival. On them trees.*
> *(turns to an exhausted Ada)*
> *You got a cider press or would that be wishing on a blessing?*

Actually, yes, I think we do.

Ruby whoops, jogs away. Ada, exhausted, takes a bite of an apple, watching her.

89. *INT. ADA'S BEDROOM, BLACK COVE FARM. PREDAWN. SUMMER 1864.*

Ada asleep. Ruby enters, shattering the calm.

RUBY

Pigs: you have any loose in the woods?

ADA

No. What? No. We bought our hams.

RUBY

There's a world more to a hog than the two hams! Lard, for example, we'll need plenty—

She picks up some discarded laundry, contemplates the overflowing laundry basket.

RUBY *(cont.)*

The catastrophe of Ada Monroe's laundry.
(marching out)
I can feel you shutting your eyes.

90. EXT. CORNFIELDS. DAY. SUMMER 1864.

Inman's walking on a track that passes through cornfields, the crop high and thick around him. He stops, hearing something. Then continues. ONCE HE'S PAST, A BODY APPEARS FROM THE CORN, THEN ANOTHER, THEN ANOTHER, ALL SLAVES ON THE RUN. ONE OF THEM HOLDS A BASKET LOADED WITH EGGS, WHICH HE

CARRIES GINGERLY. They hurry off in the opposite direction. Inman calls out:

INMAN

Hey! I'd pay a dollar for one of those eggs. Hey! Am I near the Cape Fear River?

A couple of slaves turn, look at him, then continue on their way, disappearing around the bend. Inman walks on, then hears shouts and firing, the cries of wounded men. Dogs are barking. He runs into the cover of the corn.

Horses ride by the cornfield, Home Guard, their hooves pounding the dirt track. An egg smashes on the ground in Inman's view. The dogs bring up the rear. One of them picks up Inman's scent, turns, sniffs into the corn. Starts barking. Inman runs away from the path, the corn waving his run. The dogs head into the corn. From above we see the map of the pursuit. Inman crashes through the dense, abrasive crop.

91. *EXT. CAPE FEAR RIVER. LATE DAY. SUMMER 1864.*

Inman comes to the bank of a RIVER. The water, as the light begins to go, is the color of mud, with bubbles belching to the surface, full of ugly presentiment. Inman is almost jogging now, an ear tracking his still-distant pursuers. He hears the DOGS BARKING, FAINT SHOUTS. An alligator slides into the river. There's nowhere to cross.

92. EXT. SUNKEN FOREST. DAY. SUMMER 1864.

Inman wades through A SUNKEN FOREST OF PINE, waist-deep through the filthy water to throw off the scent. He approaches a path. A figure waits, ominous. Inman sees him, goes to pull out his gun. IT'S VEASEY. His head is shaved, his face bruised and swollen, his clothes— castoffs and ill-fitting—are cinched at the waist with rope.

VEASEY

I can get you out of here.

INMAN

I should have shot you when I had the chance.

VEASEY

Please yourself. I'm just being Christian.
(*dogs bark in the distance*)
I daresay that's Home Guard following you. They're out on
the road.
(*Inman heads in the opposite direction*)
And I don't recommend that way. You'll meet half the town
coming after me with a noose. Thanks to you. I know where
there's a ferry crossing. Or you can stubborn yourself to death.

INMAN

If this is a trap . . .

Inman follows Veasey. Suspicious.

93. EXT. JETTY BY THE RIVER. LATE DAY. SUMMER 1864.

Veasey arrives at A SMALL JETTY. Inman appears, wary, negotiating the
ominous silhouettes of cypress knees.

A sign: FERRY $5. YELL LOUD.

On the far bank there's A CABIN ON STILTS above the high-water
mark. Veasey calls out. Then again.

A TINY FIGURE steps out of the cabin and waves before jumping into a
small canoe. The canoe heads against the current, the rower's back bent
with the effort. *As the canoe approaches, Veasey turns to Inman.*

VEASEY

I'm not looking for revenge, by the way. For what you did to me. No, I'm a pilgrim now, like you, traveling the road, paying our dues, relying on the kindness of strangers.

INMAN

You're nothing like me and the last thing I want right now is a conversation.

VEASEY

You might want to thank me. I could have left you to stew, same way you left me.

Now Inman sees that the ferryman is, in fact, A YOUNG GIRL, not eighteen. She calls out to them as she rows:

FERRY GIRL

You got your money?

VEASEY

(to Inman)
Five dollars.

Inman gives him a look, but produces five dollars. Veasey brandishes it as the ferry girl approaches.

VEASEY (CONT.)

Five dollars.

The ferry girl eyes the bill with contempt.

FERRY GIRL

For five dollars I wouldn't give a parched man a dipper of this river water.

INMAN

Sign says ferry, five dollars.

FERRY GIRL

This look like a ferry? My daddy's dead, or gone off to the Federals, don't matter which. I'm the way across now.

The dogs in the distance. Getting closer. Inman turns to the sound. The ferry girl is well aware of her leverage.

FERRY GIRL (CONT.)

Nobody crosses this water unless they're running from some-place. Some cross one way, some the other: makes no differ-ence, they're all running. You want to wait for your friends?

VEASEY

She's got a point.

INMAN

I can give you thirty dollars script.

FERRY GIRL

Let's go.

Shouts, more barking. Inman jumps in the canoe, and they're off. The ferry girl turns the boat around, rows them away from the jetty with the grace of someone doing something for the thousandth time.

VEASEY

(to ferry girl)
You recall Job in the scriptures? I will give free utterance to my com-plaint. I will speak in the bitterness of my soul. That's our friend here.
(to Inman)
The congregation cut off my hair. Which was hard. I was vain about my hair.
(to ferry girl)

I had curls. But I deserved it. I'm the Reverend Veasey. Have I
seen you in church?

Inman sits, scouring the bank for sign of his pursuers. The sun is sinking
fast.

FERRY GIRL

No, and you're not likely to: *I'm saving for a cowhide, and when I
get it I aim to get a saddle made, and when I get me a saddle I'll save
for a horse, and when I got a horse I'll throw on the saddle, and then
you won't see my sorry ass round this swamp again.*

*Another gurgle of viscous bubbles around the canoe, close to where Veasey's hand
flops over the side of the canoe.*

FERRY GIRL (cont.)

*You want to keep your hand in the boat. Already looks like some crit-
ter chewed his neck.*
(*she looks at Inman*)
Thirty more dollars, we can go to the cabin. I'll pull this dress
over my head.

VEASEY

(*excited*)
Have we got thirty dollars?

A SHARP SOUND, a tiny thwack of ball on meat. The ferry girl SUD-
DENLY SLUMPS BACK and falls into the water. The girl sinks quickly,
A BLOODY GAP to the side of her head. Inman, on his knees and
stretching, can't help her. They lose both oars. Then a second noise as A
HOLE THE SIZE OF A FIST appears in the canoe, just at water level.
Water pours into the canoe. Dogs bark, and now FIGURES are visible at
the jetty. HOME GUARD. Their muskets flashing. They both paddle
with their arms, heads bent low. THE GIRL'S BODY comes by them,
carried by the river, the dress billowing out, almost covering her head.
The sun has gone, the light fading, the canoe sliding downriver away
from their aggressors.

94. EXT. BOTTOM FIELD. BLACK COVE FARM. DAY. SUMMER 1864.

Ada and Ruby working with the horse to make the beginnings of A SPLIT RAIL FENCE. As they struggle with a heavy rail, Ruby is testing Ada.

RUBY

What's this wood?

ADA

I don't know. Locust?

RUBY

Where's north?

ADA

North is, north is—

RUBY

Name me three herbs growing wild on this farm.

ADA

(frustrated with Ruby and with herself)

I can't! I can't! All right? I can talk about farming in Latin. Will that do? I can read French. I know harmony and counterpoint, the Old and New Testaments. I can name the principal rivers of Europe, just don't ask me to name one stream in this county. I can embroider, but I can't darn, I can arrange cut flowers, but I can't grow them. If a thing has a function, if I might do something with it, it wasn't considered suitable.

RUBY

Why?

ADA

Ruby, you could ask why about pretty much everything to do with me.

They manage to get the first line of rail set down.

ADA (CONT.)

This fence is about the first thing I've ever done that might produce an actual result.

RUBY

So you never wrapped your legs around this Inman?

An old-fashioned look from Ada . . .

95. INT. ADA'S BEDROOM. BLACK COVE FARM. NIGHT.
SUMMER 1864

Ada, her hair plaited in a new and simpler configuration, is working on Ruby's hair while Ruby experiments with some earrings. A pile of Ada's jewelry is on the bed beside them.

ADA

Agricola poeta viam non monstrat.

RUBY

Which means?

ADA

The farmer does not point out the road to a poet.

RUBY

Which means? Should be the other way round—
(of Ada's hairdressing)

It's no wonder you're helpless and hopeless if it takes this long to fix your hair.
(of the Latin)
Say some more.

                              ADA

Terra mutata non mutat mores. A change of place does not change a character.

                              RUBY

Well, that's surely true even in English.

                              ADA

You can keep those earrings.

                              RUBY

We can't keep anything.

                              ADA

I have to keep the bangles. They were my mother's.

                              RUBY

Well, that's all. The rest is for trading. Else they can bury you in your finery.

                              ADA

(of her hair)
You're done.

There's a small mirror on a stand. It has Inman's picture stuck in it. She picks it up, removing the tintype, and holds it up for Ruby to see her hairstyle.

                              RUBY

Good God!

She takes the mirror and shows Ada her simple plait.

I like it.

RUBY

Takes two minutes. That's what I like.

She puts the earrings back in the pile.

RUBY *(cont.)*

How much do you love that piano?

96. INT. BLACK COVE, PARLOUR AND HALL, NIGHT.
SUMMER 1864.

Ada is playing the piano in the parlor. Ruby passes, on her way to bed,
stops, looks around the door to see Ada playing, with Inman's photograph
propped up in front of her. Ruby watches for a while, sways a little,
almost a dance, then makes her way up the stairs.

97. EXT. BLACK COVE FARM. DUSK. SUMMER 1864.

THE PIANO jangles down the rutted lane on the back of Mr. Roy's cart.
Ada watches, A SMALL FLOCK of sheep milling around her in the path.
Ruby is dragging a big sow toward the yard. Ada picks up one of two
sacks and staggers toward the house.

98. INT. KITCHEN, BLACK COVE FARM. DUSK. SUMMER 1864.

Ada arrives in the kitchen. They've got it under control now, scrubbed
and orderly. She puts the sack down next to another one. Her hands are
calloused, the fingernails cracked and ruined, stripes of earth under them.
Ruby comes in, struggling with the last sack, pleased.

RUBY

We're careful now, we'll get through the winter. I made old man Roy give me ten of those sheep on account of I said they were so small put together they were no bigger than six proper sheep.

ADA

My father always wanted sheep on this farm.

RUBY

I cut off my hair once, for money. My daddy got two dollars for it. Made a wig for a rich feller in Raleigh. I'm just saying, I'm real sorry you had to lose your piano.

They're working as they talk, taking the sacks into the larder, putting out stuff for the evening meal.

RUBY (CONT.)

Stobrod called himself a musician—my daddy—he could play six tunes on a fiddle. Got himself shot dead at Petersburg. I was like his goat or some creature tethered to a post. He left me once, up the mountains. I was eight. He was gone over two weeks.

ADA

Oh, Ruby.

RUBY

(defiant)

I was all right! He'd walk forty miles for liquor and not forty inches for kindness.

ADA

And your mother?

RUBY

Never met her. We're the same in that regard. He said she was—he

told me a thousand stories—she was a wolf or an Indian or a donkey.
Don't say much for him, except you know he'd be fast to work up a
sweat on a tree if he thought there was pleasure in it.

There's a pause. Ruby not easy with her emotions. Abruptly she jumps
up.

RUBY (CONT.)

There's cows to milk.

99. EXT. ANOTHER PART OF THE CAPE FEAR. EVENING.
SUMMER 1864.

In the moonlight, the canoe drifts into the muddy bank. The two men are wet and
exhausted. Inman clambers out and kneels in the mud. Veasey follows, gets to land.
And AIMS A KICK at Inman's head, knocking him back into the mud.

INMAN

Jesus, God!

VEASEY

I figure that righteous, given our history. Otherwise I'd bear a grudge
on our journey.

INMAN

There's nowhere I'm going with you except to hellfire!

100. EXT. RIVER, EN ROUTE TO SALISBURY. DAY.
SUMMER 1864.

Inman stands in the river, hoping to catch a fish, trying to concentrate.
Veasey presides, complaining . . .

VEASEY

Used to be as regular as morning prayers. Matter of fact I

could set my watch by my bowels. Open my gut now they'd find turds stacked up like little black twigs.

On a parallel track across the river, RIDERS . . . IMPOSSIBLE TO SAY WHETHER HOME GUARD OR A FEDERAL RAIDING PARTY. Inman splashes out of the water, pushes Veasey down, silencing him. The riders pass. Veasey spots something shining in the grass, picks it up. IT'S A LONG TWO-HANDED SAW.

> VEASEY (CONT.)
>
> Hey! Look at this!
> (*flexing it*)
> This is a good saw.

> INMAN
>
> (*getting up*)
> And it's not yours. You're a Christian—don't you know your commandments?

> VEASEY
>
> You'll find the good Lord very flexible on the subject of property. We could do a lot with this saw. You're going to thank me for this saw.

> INMAN
>
> I'll thank you when I've lost you and found some food. Do you ever stop talking?

Inman is vexed, walks away. Veasey follows, experimenting with the saw's music when flexed. Inman stalks on.

00. EXT. NEAR A FORD. DAY. SUMMER 1864.

Inman way ahead, full of purpose. Veasey still has the saw, trots to catch up, exasperated that Inman never waits. Inman suddenly stops, scowling, puts up a hand, listens. Inman carefully scouts the track, then, with great caution, edges toward the river bank.

A SLIGHT, PALE MAN labors in the water. He's contemplating THE HUGE BLACK CARCASS OF A BULL, which has slipped into the ford and died. The man is wet and exasperated.

> VEASEY

Good day to you!

The man turns, his spirit evidently lifted by the prospect of help. His name is JUNIOR. He's working on roping the animal.

> JUNIOR

My old bull wandered off and died in this here creek. Fouled up our water is how I found it.

Veasey is immediately an authority on bull removal. He slides down the bank, into the creek. Contemplates the carcass.

> VEASEY

This is a tricky one.

Junior offers a swig from a jug of liquor. Veasey takes a long pull, shudders happily. Inman refuses.

> VEASEY (CONT.)

The name for the Bull's member is a tassel. I learned that and never forgot it.

> JUNIOR

Reckon I need a train of mules.

> VEASEY

(walking away)
I'm getting an idea. My saw is the remedy. Let's saw up some wood and make levers.

JUNIOR

Then what?

VEASEY

(walking into the woods)
Lever him out. This'll work!

JUNIOR

Where you two sports heading?

INMAN

(inscrutable)
I don't know where he's heading. I'm going down the road.
And I got a good way to go before nightfall. So.

JUNIOR

(acknowledging his attitude)
Charitable of you to make a stop. Ain't for me to be curious.

VEASEY

(emerges from the woods)
How do you work this damn thing?

INMAN

(to Veasey)
Give me that saw.
(to Junior)
Come on.

He takes the saw, walks to the bull, gets on one side, indicates Junior
should go to the other.

INMAN (CONT.)

Let's do this in chapters.

And they begin to SAW OFF THE BULL'S NECK. Veasey looks down as a vile stew of blood and innards starts to gush into the creek. He hops back, disgusted.

> VEASEY

My, that is unpleasant!

Inman nods at Junior.

> INMAN

You might want to leave off that water for a day or two.

> JUNIOR

There'll be a tang, I'd imagine.

102. EXT. TRACK APPROACHING JUNIOR'S CABIN. EVENING. SUMMER 1864.

Junior, Inman, and Veasey come around a bend and there's A BIG CABIN LOOMING. It's in such poor repair that one end has slipped from the stones that serve as its foundation and STANDS BADLY TILTED OVER. Junior roots up another hidden jug of liquor, which he drinks from, then hands to Veasey.

> JUNIOR

There's my place. Hope you can stomach a yard chock-full of females.

> VEASEY
> (considering the wild camber)
> Looks a bit crooked.

> JUNIOR
> It is on a bit of a tilt. Them females. They all roll down one end each night!

VEASEY

—Roll me over!

JUNIOR

—In the clover!

VEASEY

—One good fart—that'll tip over!

They guffaw, delighted in the alcohol haze. Veasey suddenly exclaims, hand in the air, and rushes into the bushes.

VEASEY (CONT.)

Oh God of my God! Hallelujah! Hallelujah!

JUNIOR

What's up?

VEASEY

The Israelites! The tribes of Israel are about to flee from the banks of Egypt! Hallelujah!

INMAN

(explaining to Junior)
He's got a shit coming on. It's overdue.

JUNIOR

(bewildered)
And he's a preacher? Like a Christian?

INMAN

Like a Christian.

JUNIOR

Good God.

103. EXT. JUNIOR'S CABIN. DUSK. SUMMER 1864.

The three men arrive at the yard. DOGS AND CHILDREN MILL AROUND THE VISITORS. FOUR WOMEN COME OUT, one after the other—each of them in simple shifts that seem to emphasize their voluptuousness, or so it seems to Veasey. They frankly stare.

JUNIOR

Brought my woman home, she showed up with her three so-called sisters and their brats. The noise in that place is something awful. It's why I go hunting. These two boys is stopping for supper. They're on the road to atonement.

The women consider the men, then disappear back inside.

VEASEY

Those are fine examples of the female.

JUNIOR

Take them all and leave the saw. Be a sight more use.

SHYLA

(reappearing)
If they want to get in a tub there's an hour before food.

JUNIOR

They love to scrub a man. It's my liquor, gets their titties swinging.
(to Shyla)
Put the water on the boil.

VEASEY

(excited)
They damn!
(to Inman)
I was right about those stools—like sheep droppings—rock hard.
Quite astonishing.

104. INT. SMOKEHOUSE AT JUNIOR'S CABIN. DUSK. SUMMER 1864.

No real furniture. Veasey is shaving, whistling, settling in.

VEASEY
I think we should plan on stopping a day or two.

INMAN
I'm leaving after supper.

VEASEY
I don't know why you're in such a rush. The days pass, fat or lean, filthy or clean.

Inman gets in the tub, his back to the door. Shyla comes in, brings the kettle over to the tub, pours in the steaming water. She appraises Inman. It's intensely sexual.

SHYLA
That's battered flesh.
(of his neck wound)
I could work a finger in there.

VEASEY
He's a hero. Took that wound at Petersburg.

INMAN
He doesn't know what I am.
(uncomfortable with her stare)
Thanks.

SHYLA
(to Veasey)
He's shy, ain't he?

VEASEY
Wait up a few minutes, I'll be in that tub, then we'll see who's a shy one.

I want to poke my thumb in his holes.

A second woman comes to the door. Dolly.

DOLLY

Lila says supper's up.

105. INT. JUNIOR'S CABIN. NIGHT. SUMMER 1864.

LILA, JUNIOR'S WIFE, spoons out stew from a vast pot. The table is crammed with customers—her three sisters, the three men, the herd of dogs, and filthy children. Nobody speaks. Each time Lila bends over to spoon out of the pot, her cleavage strains against the flimsy fabric of her dress. Veasey's mesmerized. Inman is also getting drunk, his eyes increasingly glazed. When Lila makes to sit down Junior slides a hand up her dress, exposing a naked buttock, which he strokes and pinches as she pulls away.

LILA

Hey!

Junior grins, looks over at Inman, then nudges Veasey.

JUNIOR

He's gone now. Look! His eyes have gone.

INMAN

(vaguely, drunk)
What?

VEASEY

Dolly?

DOLLY

S'me.

VEASEY

Lila, Shyla, Dolly, and Mae. That's a poem. That's a poem.

He begins to recite, has a verse in his mind.

VEASEY *(cont.)*

Lila, Shyla, Dolly and Mae—
(but he can't summon it)
Da-da da-da da-da dae . . .

JUNIOR

I'm leaving soon as I'm full.

VEASEY

Really. Good bye.

JUNIOR

Got a bunch of traps needs visiting. I'll be back tomorrow, before dark. You'll still be here?

VEASEY

That's my fervent prayer.

INMAN

(suddenly)
Like to wash their hands and pray.

VEASEY

Say again?

INMAN

Lila, Shyla, Dolly, and Mae.

VEASEY

That's Job. Don't say much, but even liquored up there's a preacher in him.

Inman gets up suddenly, sways.

INMAN

I'll say my good-byes, got miles and miles to go before I reach
the Blue Ridge.
(head spinning)
I'll just quickly lie down. This house is on a bit of a tilt.

And he stumbles over to the fire, where he instantly curls up.

VEASEY

I'm heading for that smokehouse, and I'm ready to be washed
clean of my dirt.

He gets up, wanders out of the door. Junior's eyes glint. He jerks his head
toward the girls then in the direction of the smokehouse.

JUNIOR

You go tend to him.
(to Lila)
I'll be seeing you.

He picks up his gun and leaves Dolly gathering up the children and herd-
ing them out.

DOLLY

Come on, you—get!

Shyla stays, Mae having gone off after Veasey. Lila waits until the children
have gone. They consider Inman supine by the fire.

LILA

He's mine. You can go rub yourself off on the Preacher.
(of Inman)
Gonna make him hug me till I grunt.

Lila shepherds Shyla out, shuts the door, swigs from the jug, walks over to Inman, then turns to the big table and pushes pots and plates way down to one end to make a playing field. Then she bends over the prostrate Inman.

> LILA (CONT.)
>
> Hey!

Inman stirs, glazed.

> LILA (CONT.)
>
> (*kneeling down to him*)
> You want to see what Mama's got for you?

SHE SLIPS A SLEEVE OF HER DRESS TO REVEAL A FULL BREAST. Inman is drunk, doesn't think he's awake. She takes her breast to his mouth, and Inman suckles. Then she puts his hands under the dress, which rides up as his hands move between her legs. She's naked.

> LILA (CONT.)
>
> That's good. Ain't that sweet?

SHE PULLS INMAN TO HIS FEET, KISSES HIM, THEN TURNS HER BACK AND LIES FACEDOWN ON THE TABLE, HER BARE ASS UNDULATING IN THE AIR.

> LILA (CONT.)
>
> You just get on and ride me all the way to China.

He doesn't move, except to sway, eyes glazed. She turns.

> LILA (CONT.)
>
> You shy? You need a hand?
> (*goes to his buttons*)
> Let's have a look, see what we can muster.

She's kneeling now, her dress hunched up around her middle. He's in a swoon, surrendering to her, getting aroused, his hand cupping her head. THEN, AS LILA MAKES PROGRESS WITH HIS PANTS, THE BARTRAM FALLS FROM HIS BELT, SPILLING ADA'S LETTER AND TINTYPE. INMAN SURFACES, REACHES DOWN FOR IT. ON CUE, THE DOOR CRASHES OPEN AND HE'S STARING DOWN THE BARREL OF JUNIOR'S SHOTGUN.

As Lila turns, Junior KICKS HER violently in the head, knocking her over.

JUNIOR

Cover yourself up!

NEXT HE SWINGS THE SHOTGUN BARREL AGAINST THE SIDE OF INMAN'S HEAD. Inman falls back. Junior goes to the door and whistles. AND WITH THAT THE ROOM FILLS UP WITH A GROUP OF HOME GUARD BRISTLING WITH WEAPONS AND PURPOSE. THEY SEIZE INMAN, DRAG HIM OUT AS JUNIOR SPITS AND KICKS AT HIM.

106. INT. SMOKEHOUSE AT JUNIOR'S CABIN. NIGHT. SUMMER 1864.

Lila enters the smokehouse, hand to her bruised head. VEASEY'S ON THE FLOOR, WITH DOLLY ASTRIDE HIM, HIS ARM CRUSHING A NAKED MAE INTO AN EMBRACE. He considers Lila:

VEASEY

I had a special prayer you'd come visit.

THREE MEN BURST IN BEHIND HER, RIFLES RAISED.

BROWN

Get up!

107. EXT. JUNIOR'S CABIN. NIGHT. SUMMER 1864.

Veasey led out, a CHAIN GANG waiting—a bedraggled collection of prisoners, slaves, deserters—and now INMAN. Veasey is joined to the line. It starts to rain.

VEASEY
(to Junior)
God will judge you, Judas. Our lives are on your rotten soul.

108. EXT. SWANGER FARM. DAY. AUTUMN 1864.

Ruby and Ada at the door of the Swanger house. They both wear Monroe's clothes now, like brothers. THEY'RE CARRYING A SMALL SACK, A PIE UNDER A CLOTH. Ruby hammers at the door, a little impatient. Sally Swanger opens it, has to decode who it is under the clothes, the hats.

SALLY
Ada Monroe and Ruby Thewes! Look at you both!

RUBY
Look at us both what?

SALLY
Like a coupla scarecrows after a thunderstorm.

RUBY
We need a scarecrow, birds eating up half our winter garden.

ADA HOLDS UP THE PIE.

ADA
For all your kindness. Coffee. And a pie.

RUBY

That's real coffee. It ain't hickory and dirt. Found a sack hid in the larder.

SALLY

(taking the gifts)
Thank you both.
(of the pie)
Ruby, I look forward to this. We all do. Esco and me.

RUBY

(grinning at Ada)
She made it.

ADA

I made it.

SALLY

Good God in heaven.

RUBY

(by way of recommendation)
I'm still alive.

Sally's strangely awkward, lingering at the door, staring at the gifts . . .

SALLY

I know Esco's going to be real sorry he missed you . . .

They all kiss, then the girls walk back down the path. Ruby is vexed.

RUBY

That strike you as odd?

ADA

What?

RUBY

Stood at her front door?

ADA

Sally?

RUBY

Number one—I know that woman all my life, I never stood outside her house—she'd invite a wolf inside if it knocked on the door.

ADA

Perhaps, I don't know, perhaps she was busy.

RUBY

Number two—Old Man Swanger was inside that house: I could smell his pipe burning. Number three—look at these fields.

ADA

What about them?

She contemplates the stubble fields they're passing.

RUBY

We came by here a week ago, they were waist high in hay.

109. EXT. A PATH. DRIVING RAIN. NIGHT. AUTUMN 1864.

The Home Guard ride, bent under their oilskins, as the rain tips down. Between the horses, unprotected and drenched, their prisoners trudge along the muddy path. Inman and Veasey among them. Veasey has grown some beard.

AN OLDER MAN COLLAPSES, lies where he falls, not moving. There's a domino effect, and so Inman falls on top of him. He picks himself up, then tries to pull up the older man. He doesn't move.

INMAN

He's dead.

The horses plough on. Inman shouts to BROWN, the leader.

INMAN *(cont.)*

This man's dead!

Nobody pays any attention. He has to drag the body.

110. EXT. VEASEY TOWN. DAY. AUTUMN 1864.

THE HOME GUARD ESCORT THE PRISONERS PAST VEASEY'S OLD CHURCH. *More days have gone by and taken their toll on the prisoners; Veasey and Inman are haggard and filthy and reduced. The Home Guard stop for a break, chaining the prisoners to a horse rail. Citizens pass, Veasey knows them all. Some of them spit contemptuously at the deserters. None of them recognize Veasey.*

VEASEY

Am I so altered that they don't see me?

Somebody walks by with a young child. Veasey looks at Inman.

VEASEY *(cont.)*

I baptized that child.

The child stops, looks without recognizing, is tugged away from the chain gang by his mother. A slave, JOSHUA, is chained next to Veasey. He listens.

JOSHUA

And you baptized me. Put a man in chains makes him invisible.

One of the other prisoners, SHEFFIELD, leans in to Inman, his voice low.

SHEFFIELD

I'm looking to get out of this. They drag us back to fight—we're just target practice for the Federal boys.

INMAN

You run, we're all running with you, the lame and the stupid, of which we number both.

SHEFFIELD

Either way we're buggered to high hell. Run or don't run.

INMAN

Just give me some warning so I can tell the guard—I'm not getting shot again for some cause I don't believe in.

A GROUP OF SLAVES ARE WALKING BY, CARRYING SACKS. One of the women is pregnant. Veasey studies the group, sees the pregnant woman, recognizes her.

VEASEY

(mesmerized)
That's Rebecca. That's Rebecca.
(he hisses)
Rebecca!

In daylight it's apparent that Rebecca is a real beauty. She turns at the sound of her name, stops, is confused. She sees Veasey and approaches, appalled at his condition.

REBECCA

Mas?

VEASEY

Is it well with you?
(Rebecca nods)
I've been repenting for what I did. I've walked the road of atonement.

REBECCA

Your curls is all gone.

THE GUARD KICKS HIM.

GUARD

Hey!

VEASEY

(holding his head, to Rebecca)
God bless you.

Rebecca, reluctant, rejoins the other slaves, walks away with them, but then turns back to look at Veasey. She clearly cares about him. And seeing her has somehow broken his heart. He turns away from Inman, toward Sheffield.

VEASEY *(cont.)*

I'm with you. I got a baby coming.

111. EXT. HILLSIDE. DAY. AUTUMN 1864.

The chain gang, divided into two groups of six, are struggling up a hill-side. A GUARD comes running back along the track, anxious, waving wildly toward Brown.

GUARD

Federals! Cavalry! Twenty riders.

Brown swings off his horse, heads over to the chain gang and their guard, hissing orders.

BROWN

Get down! Get down!
(to their guard)
Get these sacks of shit on the ground.

Inman, Veasey are forced to lie prostrate on the bank. Brown pulls out his pistol, looks back at their horses, where an anxious GUARD is struggling to bring them under control.

> BROWN (CONT.)
>
> Hold those horses. They damn! They see us, we're dead.
> (*warning the chain gang*)
> Make a move or make a noise . . .

The Federal Cavalry are within earshot now, riding hard along the river. Now they're almost directly below the chain gang and their guards. Veasey looks at Sheffield, gets to his knees, Sheffield follows. Inman tries to pull them back down, but they're determined. There's a rattle of chains as the two men stagger to their feet. Brown hears, turns, points his pistol at Veasey, who stares, defiant, daring him to fire and draw the attention of the enemy. Sheffield tugs on the chain, pulling up the other men, including Inman. The guard struggles with Sheffield, who beats him to the ground.

> INMAN
>
> No! Don't do it!

The six men start to run along the path, the sound of their chains drowned by the thundering hooves of horses. Brown doesn't fire, he looks down as the Federals pass, calculating the risk. Then he starts to run himself, after the chain gang, another guard setting off with him, bayonet at the ready. Veasey turns, sees Brown chasing them, loses his footing as they struggle up the bank, and falls, pulling others over. Inman picks him up, practically carrying him up the slope. Brown is almost on them, sword in one hand, pistol in the other, the other guard with a bayonet fixed to his rifle. Veasey, desperate, starts to shout down to the Federals . . .

> VEASEY
>
> Hey! Hey! Hey!

The other escapees start to yell, too. ONE OF THE FEDERAL CAVALRY THINKS HE HEARS SOMETHING. He listens, yes, a shout. He yells at his fellows, turns his horse around, looks up—and a bullet catches him, sending him crashing to the ground. Now it's all out.

Brown shoots Veasey, catching him just as the gang reaches the top of the bank. They're silhouetted, like paper dolls. Veasey falls and his collapse pulls the whole gang down, each man pulling on the other, tumbling down, as Brown fires again and again into them, as does his cohort, who steps forward, stabbing with his bayonet. Inman falls, blood all over his face, his head cracking on the ground. The cohort is then shot himself, as Federals clamber up the bank, firing and fighting. Brown falls, shot in the head . . .

Next to Brown's body, the escapees lie, lifeless. Around them a firefight rages, Federals and Home Guard, but here nothing moves, nobody stirs.

112. INT. BARN, BLACK COVE FARM. DAWN. AUTUMN 1864.

Ada's milking. It's barely daylight. She's slowly becoming a country girl. Ruby appears in the doorway.

RUBY

Someone's been in the corncrib.

ADA

You sure?

RUBY

It's a coon or possum. Scratched out a fist hole in the side. This place!—I'm telling you—we grow, others eat! I'll go into town, take the last of the cider and trade for a trap.

113. EXT. THE WINTER GARDEN, BLACK COVE FARM. DAY. AUTUMN 1864.

Ada buttons Monroe's dress coat and completes the SCARECROW she's spent the day making, save for the hat, which she now fixes on, pushing in a hat pin to secure it. She's made a stern black thing and steps back to consider it. Teague appears.

> TEAGUE
>
> Scarecrow won't frighten off a Yankee. Or are you trying to make a man for yourself?

> ADA
>
> No.

> TEAGUE
>
> I come by. There's few days I don't pass by.

> ADA
>
> I know. I see you. And I don't like it.

> TEAGUE
>
> Where's your little servant girl? Trading off more of your daddy's silver? She's got her nose in the butter.
> (to his men)
> What you looking at?

114. INT. KITCHEN, BLACK COVE FARM. DAY. AUTUMN 1864.

Ada looks out at the winter garden. From that distance it really does look like her father out in the field, arms outstretched as if waiting for her to run to him. She finds it unbearable, her tears coming, runs out into the fields, attacks the scarecrow, pulling off the hat, the clothes . . .

115. EXT. HILLSIDE. MORNING. AUTUMN 1864.

A hand, pale and wet, protrudes from the mound of bodies of the murdered chain gang.

SOMETHING SHIFTS. Inman—wedged under three or four corpses—their limbs and chains wrapped around him, has regained consciousness. He coughs, can't breathe properly, tries to work himself some air, spitting out dirt. He makes a noise to distract the goat, rattling the chains. Inman struggles to move, the bodies slithering off him, but even then the animal only retreats a yard or two. VEASEY SLIDES FACE UP, A BULLET IN HIS FOREHEAD LIKE A MYSTICAL THIRD EYE. Inman feels a surprising loss and tenderness.

116. *EXT. OLD MILL, COLD MOUNTAIN. DAY.*
AUTUMN 1864.

Ruby rides back from town along the river. An ugly-looking trap is tied over the horse, and three or four bulging sacks. By AN ABANDONED MILL she sees the Home Guard under the trees.

> TEAGUE
>
> *What you looking to catch?*

> RUBY
>
> *What?*

> TEAGUE
>
> *With that trap.*

> RUBY
>
> *We got some critter stealing our corn.*

> TEAGUE
>
> *Still but the two of you up there, is it?*

> RUBY
>
> *You know it.*

TEAGUE

When we get a cold night, camped out, trying to maintain the rule of
law, protecting girls like you from Yankees and deserters, that's a
thought warms us—
(to his men)
ain't it?—the two of you up there on my grandpappy's farm, dressed
in men's clothes. Warms us right up. What you got in the sacks?
(to the men)
Looks like human heads! Eh? Looks like a bunch of heads. We got
competition!

Ruby rides on. She rides around the bend—she's not far from the Swanger farm.

117. EXT. SWANGER FARM. DAY. AUTUMN 1864.

*Sally is washing sheets. Ruby rides up. Sally seems a little vexed to see her. She
walks down to the gate.*

SALLY

Ruby—

RUBY

I'm not stopping, Sally. I'm not snooping neither. Just you should
know Teague and his boys are lurking down at Pigeon River, by the
Old Frazier Mill.

SALLY

(after a beat)
You tell Ada that was a good pie.

*Ruby rides off. Sally watches, then goes inside the house, her energy changing
immediately, as if she might faint.*

118. EXT. BOTTOM FIELD, BLACK COVE FARM. DAY.
AUTUMN 1864.

Ruby rides up to the farm. She admires THE SCARECROW—WHICH NOW PARODIES ADA, the same outfit she once wore to visit Inman, the same dress, same hat. Ada comes over.

> RUBY

The hat's a nice touch.

They start unloading sacks.

> RUBY *(cont.)*

You're quiet.

> ADA

I cried for my daddy. I dressed up the scarecrow in his suit and he came back, his arms out, said you never cried enough, you never cried enough.

> RUBY

Well, now you did.

> ADA

Then I thought, it's not my daddy, it's my sweetheart. I saw him once that way, when I looked down Sally's well. So I dressed the scarecrow in the dress I wore the day he left. In case his spirit flies over, looking out for me.
(of the vicious-looking trap)
That looks terrible.

Ruby opens the sacks.

> ADA *(cont.)*

Cabbages.

> RUBY

I bargained like Lucifer. We can make all kinds of good eating.

ADA

Such as?

RUBY

Cabbage, slaw, sauerkraut, cabbage soup, fried cabbage, stuffed cabbage . . .

119. EXT. SWANGER FARM. DAY. AUTUMN 1864.

Sally is pinning out white sheets, they're filling out like sails in the afternoon wind. TEAGUE'S MEN RIDE UP TO THE FARM. Esco's out in the field, laboring away, but with his shotgun by him. Teague stops alongside the field, the rail between him and Esco. Esco stops working, picks up his shotgun, and goes over, shooing Sally indoors. Teague has four men with him. MO and JO, the twins, huge, and with the appearance of having less than one brain between the two of them, GRAYLING, a reluctant-looking man, funereal in his bearing, and BOSIE.

TEAGUE

Afternoon.

The riders slowly fan out, almost as if choreographed.

ESCO

Don't spread out. Why they spreading out?

TEAGUE

I'm not spreading out, I'm sitting here.

Esco comes over the rail fence, his gun loose in his hands.

TEAGUE (CONT.)

Never knew a man worked in his field with a shotgun.

ESCO

There's a war on.

Teague fishes in his coat. Esco's gun swings up. Teague shows him a cigar case, shrugs, puts a cheroot in his mouth.

120. INT. SWANGER FARM. DAY. AUTUMN 1864.

From inside the house, Sally watches everything. Her view impaired by the sheets.

121. EXT. SWANGER FARM. DAY. AUTUMN 1864.

Mo dismounts. Ambles past Esco, looks behind the sheets. ESCO KICKS OUT AT HIM, the shotgun rigid and pointing.

> ESCO
>
> Get off my land.

Mo examines his breeches for a dust mark, wipes it off, retreating in a turkey walk of examining and dusting.

> TEAGUE
>
> Your boys come back.

> ESCO
>
> Ain't seen my boys in four years. They're fighting other boys, not old men and women.

> TEAGUE
>
> (*to his men*)
> He means us. He's referring there to us.
> (*to Esco*)
> So you won't care if we take a look around?

> ESCO
>
> What I gotta give you? A chicken? A lamb?

TEAGUE

(shrugs)

Sure. Thing is—you got one barrel and there's five of us. Not a fair fight.

BOSIE SUDDENLY DROPS OFF HIS HORSE, ROLLS ON THE GROUND.

BOSIE

King of Kings!

Esco is momentarily distracted, and in that instant, Mo kicks out at him, knocking the gun from his hands, which fires into the air, a shocking sound.

122. EXT. BLACK COVE FARM. DAY. AUTUMN 1864.

Ruby and Ada digging a trench by the smokehouse, laying in the pale heads of cabbage. They hear the distant shot.

RUBY

What's that?

They stop. Listen. Look at each other, start running.

123. EXT. SWANGER FARM. DAY. AUTUMN 1864.

Jo sets on Esco, knocking him backward into a sheet, where it gets twisted, while Jo kicks and punches, little spots of blood staining the sheet with each blow. MO PULLS OUT HIS SABER AND RUNS ESCO THROUGH, LEAVES THE SABER IN DEEP, PINNING ESCO TO THE SHEET, THEN SPINS HIM AROUND IN THE SHEET SO THAT IT TIGHTENS. A stain grows out from the blade, huge and spreading. Teague walks up to Esco.

TEAGUE

You're harboring deserters. I can confiscate this farm and everything on it, every plate, every sheet, every little pellet of chicken shit—I can confiscate your old lady's asshole, so don't offer me a bird.

Sally runs out, screaming. She tries to pull out the saber. MO REVERSES HIS RIFLE AND CLUBS HER TO THE GROUND.

TEAGUE (cont.)

(sharply)
Hey!

Mo backs away. Sally is screaming. She watches, helpless, as Esco dies in front of her, the sheet growing a darker red.

TEAGUE (cont.)

You got your bait. Set it on the hook.

BOSIE, SMILING, FETCHES A ROPE FROM HIS HORSE, ALREADY NOOSED AT ONE END. HE FLIPS THE LOOP OVER SALLY'S HEAD.

124. INT. BARN, SWANGER FARM. DAY. AUTUMN 1864.

ELLIS AND ACTON SWANGER emerge from their hiding places, unable to bear the sound of their mother's screams. They're carrying an axe and a pitchfork, mad for revenge.

125. EXT. SWANGER FARM. DAY. AUTUMN 1864.

BOSIE IS DOING SOME SORT OF DANCE ALONG THE FENCE RAIL. He's very graceful, his hair flying, his hands out, one fingernail extremely long, his boots stamping down on the fence.

UNDER HIS STOMPING FEET, THE RAIL POST IS PRESSED ON
SALLY SWANGER'S THUMBS.

She can't scream any longer, because the noose has practically strangled
her. The rope's tied off to Bosie's horse, which yanks on the noose with
every slight movement. Sally is prostrate in the dirt.

Her two boys come running from the barn. TEAGUE CASUALLY
SHOOTS ELLIS WITH HIS RIFLE. BOSIE LETS ACTON GET ALL
THE WAY TOWARD HIM AND THEN SHOOTS HIM FROM A
YARD AWAY, THE GUN SUDDENLY SPRINGING INTO HIS
HAND. AS ACTON FALLS, BOSIE DOES A FLIP TO DIVE OFF THE
POST AND LAND ON HIS FEET NEXT TO ACTON'S BODY.

126. EXT. HILLSIDE. MORNING. AUTUMN 1864.

INMAN begins inching along the ground, the chain of dead bodies in
tow, a macabre tug-of-war. He encounters some goats. They consider
him. TWO LEGS COME INTO VIEW, THEN THE BARREL OF A
GUN.

127. EXT. MADDY'S CARAVAN. AFTERNOON. AUTUMN 1864.

HARSH WHISTLES. A secret place, in the heart of a forest. There's the
answering sound of SMALL BELLS, a chorus of them. Inman is dragged
into view on a makeshift litter. Goats appear; they herd around the figure
dragging the litter. IT'S AN OLD WOMAN, silver-haired, her face a
leather map, her clothes leather, everything about her like old leather.
HER NAME IS MADDY.

She drags Inman around a bend and there's her house—AN OLD CARA-
VAN, long grown into the ground and plaited with vines and creepers.
*Inman tries to sit up. An old whiskered BILLY GOAT butts up against Inman,
knocks him down. Maddy pays no attention to the struggle, heads inside her caravan.*

MADDY

Mind that Billy, he's the jealous kind.

She emerges with a bowl of water and rags, and washes his face, pushing back his hair to look at his wound, putting a finger to the gash on his neck, professional in her appraisal. Inman is barely conscious. He groans, trying to defend himself.

MADDY (cont.)

Pay no attention to me. What happened to your head?

INMAN

Fighting.

MADDY

And your neck?

INMAN

Different fighting.

MADDY

You're the color of a cadaver. I'll fix you. I can fix you up.

INMAN

(speaking of his spirit)
Mister—you could fix me, I'd be in your everlasting debt.

MADDY

Debts, fighting—them words don't mean much round here. For the record, I'm a female of the species.

128. EXT. SWANGER FARM. DUSK. AUTUMN 1864.

Ada and Ruby, riding together on the horse, arrive at the Swangers. SALLY IS STILL PINNED UNDER THE FENCE POST. The noose around her neck has been tied off to the post so that she can't move. Ada goes to Esco. Ruby heaves at the fence.

I can't get this damn thing off her.

Ada, I can't get this off her!

Ada runs over. They struggle, manage to raise the rails. Sally's lips are moving.

RUBY (CONT.)

What darling? What?

She bends down, loosening the noose. Looks up at Ada.

RUBY (CONT.)

She's saying don't bother. This world won't stand long. God won't let it stand this way long.

129. INT. MADDY'S CARAVAN. DAY. AUTUMN 1864.

An exotic interior, many crocks and jars, bunches of herbs, wrapped papers of dried things, like a woodland apothecary store. Inman wakes up. He finds himself in a small cot, wrapped in blankets, a poultice at his neck. He doesn't know where he is or how long he's been there.

130. EXT. MADDY'S CARAVAN. DAY. AUTUMN 1864.

Maddy's sitting on a stool. There's a circle of stones where her fire lives and she sets the tinder to it. Inman emerges from the caravan. He's pale and unsteady. Maddy calls over a little goat. It ambles over affectionately and nuzzles into her hand. She strokes it and scratches under the chin. The creature becomes increasingly tranquil.

INMAN

How long have I been sleeping?

MADDY

Two days, three days. Not long enough.

INMAN

I can't stop here. I'm a deserter. They find me here things could be bad for you.

MADDY

What they going to do? Cut short my young life? Sit down before you fall down.

The goat looks as if it has fallen asleep.

MADDY (CONT.)

I've learned a person can pretty much survive off of a goat. I can't abide a chicken, but a goat gives you company and milk and cheese and then, when you need it, good meat.

In a single motion she has a knife in her hand and has SLIT THE THROAT OF THE GOAT, putting the bowl underneath its neck to catch the blood, still stroking the goat, which blinks as if it were only surprised, and not dying.

MADDY (CONT.)

So you've been fighting?

INMAN

(as if he might break)
I could be at killing for days sometimes, in the hand to hand, my feet against the feet of my enemy, and I always killed him and he never killed me.

MADDY

He gave it a try, to look at you.

INMAN

I guess he did.

MADDY

See, I think there's a plan. There's a design. For each and every
one of us.

During this she's shucking the skin off the goat with the authority of
someone who's done this a thousand times.

MADDY (CONT.)

You look at nature, a bird flies somewhere, picks up a seed,
shits the seed out, a plant grows. Bird's got a job, shit's got a
job, seed's got a job.

131. INT. MADDY'S CARAVAN. EVENING. AUTUMN 1864.

A wood-burning stove with a single cooking plate—on which pieces of
the goat meat, sprinkled with herbs, are sizzling in a pan. INMAN IS
EATING LIKE A MAN POSSESSED, WRAPPING THE MEAT IN
CORN FRITTERS AND PUSHING THEM INTO HIS MOUTH.
Maddy watches him, adds another mound of meat to his plate. Inman
nods in thanks, but doesn't look up.

*She opens a jar and takes out a handful of dried poppy heads, puts them near the
stove, then dips into another jar and pulls out what look like old cheroot stubs.*

MADDY

Take one of these now with your food.

Inman is circumspect, views the stub lozenge with suspicion.

MADDY (cont.)

Swallow it. If you die I'll give you your money back.

*Inman puts it in his mouth, gags at the taste of it. She hands him a beaker with
milk to wash it down.*

Our minds aren't made to hold on to the particulars of pain, the way we do bliss.

She starts steaming the poppies.

INMAN

It's true.

MADDY

What is?

INMAN

What you remember.

MADDY

What's her name?

INMAN

Ada—
(at the food.)
Sometimes I think I'm crazy when I'm just hungry.
(another mouthful)

Maddy pricks open the poppies and collects their opium, then hands Inman the liquid.

MADDY

Now drink this, it visits the pain and you'll sleep. And is she waiting for you? This Ada Monroe?

INMAN

She was. I don't know. Or if she'd know me. I'm like the boy who goes out in winter for firewood, comes back in the spring with a whistle.

He drinks the laudanum she's made. She dips a cloth in the steaming water, unbuttons his shirt. She has a crock of what looks like treacle and Vaseline. She smears this salve over the neck wound, into his scalp. Inman surrenders to the drug.

INMAN (CONT.)
The passenger pigeons fly south, the berries ripen. Whether I see them or not, whether a man dies, or a war is won.

MADDY
That's the laudanum getting to you. That's good. Say something more.

He obliges as she gets to work on his wrists, where the chain has chewed into the flesh.

INMAN
She gave me a book. Ada Monroe. Man by the name of Bartram. Wrote about his travels. I carried that book through every battle. Through all my walking. Her picture in it. Sometimes just reading the name of a place near home— Sorrell Cove, Fire Scald Ridge. Thing is, I've been thinking— those places belonged to people before us, to the Indian. What did he call Cold Mountain? How can a name not even the real name break your heart? It's her, she's the place I'm heading. And I hardly know her. So how can a person who's maybe not even a real person—I don't know what I'm talking about—I have to close my eyes . . .

He slides off the stool and lies on the floor. Maddy finds a blanket, which she drapes over him.

ADA (V.O.)
To have traveled so far, a thousand terrible miles . . .

132. INT. MONROE'S BEDROOM, BLACK COVE FARM. DAY. AUTUMN 1864.

Ada is reading from the Bartram book to Sally, who is propped up in Monroe's old bed.

> ADA
>
> . . . over all God's surfaces, His oceans, His swamps, His slopes and ridges, to find myself at last, a mark in the aching snow from whence I beheld a sublimely awful scene of power and majesty, a world of mountains piled upon mountains—

> RUBY (O.S.)
>
> Ada! Hey, Ada!

Ada closes the book and opens the window. Ruby is out in the yard with a shotgun and a determined look.

> RUBY (CONT.)
>
> It's a man.

> ADA
>
> What is?

> RUBY
>
> Raiding our corn. Got him in the trap. That's him yelping.

> ADA
>
> You're not going to shoot him!

> RUBY
>
> I don't want him to shoot me.
> *(of the gun)*
> Can you fire this thing?

ADA

(*making it clear she can't*)
Yes.

133. EXT. YARD, BLACK COVE FARM. DAY. AUTUMN 1864.

Ruby and Ada head toward the corncrib, bundled up against the cold.

A MAN IS KNEELING AT THE CORNCRIB, perfectly caught in the art of stealing, his head forced away from view. Ruby hands Ada the gun and approaches, warily.

RUBY

Listen up—you got a barrel trained on your rear end.

STOBROD

Get me out of this dang thing. My fist's about to drop off.

RUBY

You got a weapon?

STOBROD

No ma'am. I'm begging you. I'm already on my knees, otherwise I'd get down on them.

RUBY

(*suddenly recognizes the voice*)
Unbelievable! Stobrod Thewes.

STOBROD

Ruby? They damn!

ADA

What?

RUBY

(to Ada, disgusted)
That's my daddy . . .

She walks up to him and KICKS HIM AS HARD AS SHE CAN ON HIS
BACKSIDE.

134. INT. KITCHEN, BLACK COVE FARM. DAY. AUTUMN 1864.

A strip of fabric, a homemade bandage, is being wrapped around Stobrod's
badly gashed hand. Ada is tending to him. Ruby is cooking at the range,
not remotely warm toward her prodigal father, who looks rather comfortable. Stobrod looks at her.

STOBROD

Just so's you know—I can eat while she's doing this . . .

RUBY

Just so's you know—you're not eating inside. Number One—
they hang people round here for taking in deserters. Number
two—even if they gave out prizes, you'd still eat outside.

STOBROD

You're scarred.

RUBY

I'm what?

STOBROD

Your heart. Scarred. I did wrong to you.

RUBY

You'd be scarred. You'd be really scarred if I hadn't wrapped
them trap teeth in sacking.

Which was my idea.

RUBY

Which was her idea.

STOBROD

I hurt you.

RUBY

Good God!

STOBROD

I wrote fifty tunes with you in mind. Ruby this, Ruby that,
Ruby with the eyes that sparkle.

RUBY

Hey! Let's agree: you beat me, you abandoned me, you ignored
me, you beat me some more—all of that is better than Ruby
with the eyes that sparkle!

STOBROD

I'm changed. People change. War changes people something
terrible.
(to Ada)
Ruby's told you—I've no doubt—I wasn't always the best . . .

RUBY

You were an asshole.

STOBROD

I can't disagree with that. I was.

RUBY

Get him out of here!

STOBROD

Music's changed me. I'm full of music, darling. I wish I'd brung my fiddle—Hey Ruby! Got a new fiddle—it's got a little snake's rattle in the body—took it off a dead Federal in Virginia. It's a beautiful fiddle. It's full of tunes, Ruby. I didn't know I had it in me. Don't know if it's from that little rattle locked up in it, or from something untied my heart.

Ruby walks over with a crock, wrapped in a cloth.

RUBY

You're all set.

STOBROD

(sincerely)
Bless you both.

He goes to the door.

RUBY

Ain't you got a proper coat?

STOBROD

Darling, I'm fine. And you just say the word, I won't come back, neither. I don't want to put either you or your mistress here in any bother.

ADA

I'm not Ruby's employer.

STOBROD

Oh, beg pardon.

RUBY

Nobody is.
(Stobrod digests this)

I'll make up food for you, you come Sundays before it's light,
I'll leave it behind the Old Frazier Mill.

                    STOBROD
Do you know who really needs a coat, darling, is my partner,
fat boy name of Pangle. We're hiding up in the caves with a
singer, name of Georgia, and he feels the cold like a thin man,
but ain't no coat'll fit him.
(leaving)
I love you, Ruby. In case the sky falls on our head. You're a
good girl.

And he's gone. Ruby scowls. FIDDLE MUSIC BEGINS.

                    RUBY
He is so full of manure, that man, we could lay him on the dirt
and grow another one just like him.

                    ADA
So that's Stobrod Thewes.

                    RUBY
It is, and that's the last you'll see of him.

135. EXT. MADDY'S CARAVAN. DUSK. AUTUMN 1864.

THE FIDDLE CONTINUES, A BANJO JOINS IN. Maddy is loading
up Inman for his journey. She hands him a bulging goatskin satchel.

                    MADDY
That's medicine and goat meat. You're sick of both.

                    INMAN
I have a deal to thank you for.

She hands him an ancient flintlock pistol.

And that's just for show.

She turns, abruptly, mingles in with her goats. Inman nods, knows that she doesn't want a fuss, although he wants to make one, and turns himself, heads away from the caravan.

136. INT. RUBY'S ROOM, BLACK COVE FARM. DAWN. AUTUMN 1864.

THE MUSIC CONTINUES. Ruby wakes up. Looks out of the window. Ada, also woken, comes into Ruby's room. STOBROD IS OUTSIDE WITH PANGLE, FIDDLE AND BANJO. Ruby opens the window, scowling. Stobrod beams, stops playing, holds up the food, points at Pangle in his new coat. Pangle waves.

RUBY

Get on back where you came from!

Stobrod and Pangle smile and hurry away.

147. EXT. PATH IN HILL COUNTRY. DAY. WINTER 1864.

WINTER SETTING IN. Inman, increasingly a stick figure in the landscape, wasted and fragile, trudges along through fallen leaves in a rocky riverbed. He unwraps a paper containing the last scraps of goat meat. He walks and eats, fishes out a lozenge, tries to swallow it, washes it down with a drink from his flask. Opens the crock of salve and rubs the treacly grease into his neck and ankle.

ADA (V.O.)

"My love for Linton is like the foliage in the woods. Time will change it like winter changes the trees. My love for Heathcliff resembles the eternal rocks beneath—"

138. INT. ADA'S BEDROOM, BLACK COVE FARM. NIGHT. WINTER 1864.

Ada in the bed, reading to Ruby from *Wuthering Heights*.

> ADA
>
> —a source of little visible delight. But necessary.

> RUBY
>
> She ain't gonna marry Linton, is she? She said—whatever our souls are made of, his and mine are the same. You can't say that about Heathcliff and then marry Linton.

> ADA
>
> We'll find out.
> *(sleepy)*
> Tomorrow.

> RUBY
>
> I'm not waiting until tomorrow.

> ADA
>
> Ruby, I'm falling asleep.

She lies back in her bed. Ruby takes the book, lies across the bottom of the bed, as Ada goes to sleep.

> RUBY
>
> Little visible delight, but necessary. I like that . . .

139. EXT. SMALL WOOD. NIGHT. WINTER 1864.

DRIVING RAIN. Inman shelters under a huge tree whose split trunk provides a mean shelter. He inserts himself into the cleft of it, a black thing in a black tree, like a troll. He stands, shivers, sodden, desolate.

140. INT. OLD MILL, COLD MOUNTAIN. CHRISTMAS DAY.
NIGHT. WINTER 1864.

THE MUSIC CONTINUES. Stobrod is playing the fiddle, his bowing
hand still lightly taped and a fingerless mitten covering it. They're in the
abandoned mill, a derelict space, which has been cheered up with some
rudimentary Christmas decorations. Ada, Ruby, and Sally Swanger, her
hair now almost completely white, are there. Some token presents. Pangle
is picking at a banjo, his grin infectious, and there's a third player,
GEORGIA. As they play:

PANGLE

(of Sally)
She don't speak.

STOBROD

She can't speak. I told you.

PANGLE

(smiles at Sally)
Is she feeble then?

STOBROD

No.
(to Sally)
Don't mind him.
(to Ruby)
Hey Ruby: what about this?

He starts the tune of "Wayfaring Stranger." Ruby groans.

STOBROD (cont.)
Don't make that face—you listen: c'mon Georgia . . .

141. EXT. SARA'S CABIN. NIGHT. WINTER 1864.

A LITTLE CABIN. Its lights coming through square windows like a Chinese lantern. Inman considers it, the risk versus the shelter. The sleet still pelts down on him and he decides to approach. Closer, he can hear a sound coming from the house. IT'S A BABY'S INCESSANT CRY. HE SEES A YOUNG WOMAN WALKING AROUND AND AROUND IN THE ROOM, CLUTCHING THE BABY WRAPPED UP IN A QUILT.

Inman knocks hard on the door. The light from the lamp goes out, although the fire still gives the room a clear glow.

INMAN

I'm one man alone. I'm a Confederate soldier on furlough. I have no bad intention. I need shelter and food.

THE TINY SOUND OF THE DOOR BEING BOLTED.

INMAN (CONT.)

Can I at least sleep in the corncrib—just for some shelter? I'll be on my way come morning.

No answer. Inman accepts this as a rebuttal, and trudges back toward the road.

SARA (V.O.)

I've got a rifle.

Inman turns. A gap in the door appears.

INMAN

Fair enough.

The baby's crying behind the woman.

SARA

There's some beans and corn pone, all I got. You better come in.

142. INT. SARA'S CABIN. NIGHT. WINTER 1864.

Inman enters the cabin. It's a single room. A big fire. The baby on the bed, a rudimentary crib unoccupied next to it. The woman is already at the little stove. She turns to him. She's young, tiny, painfully beautiful. Inman, despite himself, is mesmerized.

> INMAN

Thank you.

> SARA

I'm alone here, as you can see, with my baby. I need to believe you mean no harm.

Inman takes out Maddy's flintlock. She starts, terrified.

> INMAN

No, I mean to give it to you.

He turns it handle forward and offers it to her.

> SARA

I don't want it. I had my way they'd take metal altogether out of this world. Every blade, every gun.

He places the pistol on the mantelpiece.

> INMAN

Is your baby sick?

> SARA

He cries. I don't know. He cries a lot. My man is dead. He took his wound at Gettysburg. Never saw his boy.

She never once looks at him. Her eyes on the floor or the food or the baby.

INMAN

I'm sorry.

SARA

It's pretty much what you'll get if you knock on any door of this war. Man dead, woman left.

She hands him a plate of steaming beans. An onion perched on top.

SARA (CONT.)

It's mean food but it's hot.

She goes over to the bed and picks up her baby and starts the same business of walking him, singing the while an odd lament. Inman eats, looks at her, at the child and the fire. He picks up the onion, bites into it. Sara looks across.

INMAN

(ashamed of his hunger)

There's no hunting on the road, just cress and—

He takes another bite.

SARA

I need to feed this man.

Inman turns his back to her. He sits finishing the food while she puts the baby to her breast, slipping the shoulder from her dress. *While the baby feeds:*

SARA (cont.)

Used to have a cow, few goats. Raiders took them. Made me kill our own dog on the porch. That poor creature watched over me. Nothing left now save a hog and a couple of chickens to live off till spring. I'll have to kill that hog and make sense of the flesh and divisions— which is something I never did.

INMAN

I could do that for you in the morning.

SARA

He won't feed. I'm not asking.

INMAN

It's what I'd gladly do for you for what you're gladly doing for me.
I'm Inman, by the way. That's my name.

SARA

I'm Sara. My baby's Ethan.

INMAN

Glad to know you both.

143. EXT. SARA'S CABIN. NIGHT. WINTER 1864.

Sara walks ahead of Inman. She carries a pile of clothing, a pair of boots.
It's still wretched outside. She hugs the side of the house, the porch barely
offering shelter. INMAN FOLLOWS, with a bowl of steaming water and
a small towel over his arm. She hands him the clothes.

SARA

You look about his size. He was another man straight up and
down.

There's a palpable attraction between them, so that every exchange seems
to contain a promise, a sexual charge.

INMAN

Thank you.

She sets down the lantern and leaves. By its dim light, Inman peels off his
clothes, sets to work with the bar of soap and the cloth to scrub himself

clean. He can be seen from the window and finds himself turning away to pull off his pants.

144. INT. SARA'S CABIN. NIGHT. WINTER 1864.

Sara sits at the cot, still singing to the baby, then gets up, goes to the window, sees Inman dressing, walks to the door, lets it open a little, but not so as she can be seen.

> SARA
>
> They fit?

> INMAN (O.S.)
>
> Pretty much. These boots are good boots.

> SARA
>
> I'll say good night.

> INMAN (O.S.)
>
> Good night.

145. EXT. SARA'S CABIN. NIGHT. WINTER 1864.

Inman settles down into the corncrib. He's cold and everything is damp and lumpy and uncomfortable. He pulls his thin blanket around him. The wind is howling. He levers himself up, looks at the house with its warm invitation, can almost feel Sara in there. He reluctantly settles down again. HE HEARS A NOISE, STEPS APPROACHING.

> SARA
>
> Will you come inside?

She stands in a shift, a blanket over her shoulders. Her body under the cotton very clear to him. She turns, goes back inside.

146. INT. SARA'S CABIN. NIGHT. WINTER 1864.

Inman comes in. Sara is sitting on her bed. Long silence.

SARA

Could you do something for me? Do you think you could lie here, next to me, and not need to go further?

INMAN

I don't know. I'll try.

He sits on the bed as she slips under the covers, and then removes the boots, his shirt, gets under the covers. There's an electric space between them. Then Sara begins to cry, pulls his arm to open up so that she can be folded into him. SHE SOBS, SHUDDERING IN THE BED.

INMAN (CONT.)

I'll go. I'll go, shall I?

SARA

I don't want you to.

INMAN

Thing is, I love someone. I love someone very much.

They lie, staring up at the ceiling, her tears falling. A FIDDLE PLAYS.

147. INT. OLD MILL, COLD MOUNTAIN. CHRISTMAS DAY. NIGHT. WINTER 1864.

GEORGIA BEGINS TO SING. He's like a pale angel and sings with a soft, true voice. Ruby finds herself taken by this boy's voice and by Stobrod's extraordinary invention as he takes the tune off on a wild journey. Ruby sits next to Ada, fiddles with her bracelets, slips one from Ada's wrist and slides it over her own.

148. EXT. OLD MILL, COLD MOUNTAIN. EVENING.
WINTER 1864.

They're all outside now, shaking hands.

                    GEORGIA

There's snow in the air.

                    RUBY

Don't sleep here.

                    STOBROD

We won't.

                    ADA

It's bitter, they could stop one night.

                    RUBY

They stop one night, they'll want to stop two.

                    PANGLE

This coat's warm.

                    STOBROD

What about next Sunday? That'll be the New Year. It's gonna
be a better one.

                    RUBY

Maybe.

                    GEORGIA

The war's over in a month.

                    RUBY

He said that a month ago.

ADA

(shaking Stobrod's hand in good night)
It started off being over in a month.

STOBROD

Miss Ada. Merry Christmas.

ADA

Merry Christmas. Pangle. Georgia.

GEORGIA

'Night.

PANGLE

'Night now.

The three women walk down the lane, the three men watch.

PANGLE (CONT.)

I like my coat. It's a good coat.

STOBROD

That's my Ruby.

GEORGIA

She's an original.

STOBROD

You think the good Lord would forgive an old cold fool if he
changed his mind? Ada said it herself it was bitter . . .

149. EXT. SWANGER FARM. NIGHT. WINTER 1864.

The three women head toward Sally's house.

RUBY

What kind of name's Georgia?

ADA

It's where he comes from, it's not his name.

RUBY

I know that's meant to be the ugliest state under the heavens.

ADA

Why do you care what his name is?

RUBY

(a funny look, then)
What's that cluster of stars?

ADA

Orion.

RUBY

What about them shaped like a wishbone?

ADA

That's Taurus the bull, and that's Gemini, and that's Orion's big dog, Canis Major.

RUBY

Listen to her, Sal. She's turned into a highland girl.

ADA

I could always name the stars, Ruby, that was never my problem.

They all three have linked arms. Ada imitates Stobrod.

ADA (CONT.)

I love you, darling. In case that big old sky falls on our heads.
And I love you, too, Sally.

RUBY

It's sad, Sal. It's a c-a-t-a-s-t-r-o-p-h-e.

150. INT. SARA'S CABIN. EARLY. WINTER 1864.

Sara, dressed, agitated—the baby already complaining—is urgently shaking Inman, hissing at him:

SARA

Get out of here, quick!

Inman surfaces from deep sleep.

SARA (CONT.)

Yankees are coming. They find you here, it'll go bad on all of us.

Inman is up, grabbing clothes, boots, knapsack.

INMAN

I can try and fight them.

SARA

No, my baby. Please no! Just get.

She pulls up the window in back of the cabin. Inman throws things out into the freezing morning. He swings over the window and down onto the frosty ground.

151. EXT. SARA'S CABIN. EARLY. WINTER 1864.

Inman picks up his stuff and, at a crouch, runs for cover to the wood that borders the property. He can hear horses and a commotion at the front of Sara's cabin, but doesn't look around until he's sheltered by the trees.

FEDERAL SOLDIERS, a raiding party, have dismounted and are approaching the cabin. Inman watches, pulling on his shirt, then HE REALIZES HE DOESN'T HAVE A WEAPON.

One of the soldiers, PISTOL, has dragged Sara from the cabin. A second soldier, NYM, emerges carrying Ethan. Sara starts up, struggles with him, is knocked down. INMAN HAS TO WATCH AS THEY DRAG HER OVER TO A FENCE POST AND ROPE HER TO IT, THEN SLIP THE BLANKET OFF THE BABY AND LAY IT ON THE GROUND IN THE MIDDLE OF THE YARD. Then Sara starts to scream.

Inman is dressed. Boots on. He looks back at the yard. The men sitting, smoking, prepared to wait, their breath coming out in gusts in the freezing air. Flakes of snow fall.

PISTOL

We got all day.
(*indicating the chickens*)
Them birds won't get you through winter.

SARA

My baby's sick! Cover him up! He's shaking! Have mercy. I got a hog! He's hid out back.

A third Federal, BARDOLPH, young, decent, a reluctant participant, chases after the chickens, gathers them up. PISTOL goes for the hog.

SARA (CONT.)

I got nothing else. I swear.

Nym gets close to her, putting his rifle to her chest.

NYM

That ain't necessarily so. You're a pretty little thing.

SARA

Yes! Take me inside! Let's all go inside! Take my baby inside
and then we'll do whatever you want.

Nym unties her. Pistol has a rope around the hog and now leads it toward
the horses. Sara cries out:

SARA (CONT.)

You take that hog I'm as good as dead. Cover up my boy!

She's wailing, an unbearable ululation. NYM SLAPS HER, TWICE,
HARD.

152. INT. SARA'S CABIN. DAY. WINTER 1864.

The door is kicked open. Nym pushes Sara inside, kicks the door shut,
REVEALING INMAN STANDING BEHIND IT.

153. EXT. SARA'S CABIN. DAY. WINTER 1864.

Bardolph, a chicken in his arms, goes over to the baby.

BARDOLPH

This is ready to get a fit going.

PISTOL

What do you care?

BARDOLPH

It's shuddering. It's gone blue.

PISTOL

(*calling to Nym*)

Hey! Leave some for the rest of us.

Pistol heads towards the cabin. As he approaches the door, Bardolph rearranges the blankets to cover the baby. Pistol opens the door. Nym is on top of Sara. Pistol laughs, enters, and is clubbed down by Inman, who steps out onto the porch while SARA SHRUGS OFF THE BODY OF NYM, HIS THROAT CUT.

Bardolph looks up to see Inman walking towards him, carrying Pistol's Colt revolver. Bardolph has left his weapon by the fence.

INMAN

Move away from the baby.

Bardolph obeys, terrified. Sara runs out, collects Ethan, gives a little moan of anguish, runs back inside the cabin.

BARDOLPH

Don't shoot.

INMAN

Take off your boots.

(*Bardolph does so*)

Take off your pants, and your shirt.

BARDOLPH

Don't shoot me, please. We're starving. We haven't eaten in days.

INMAN

You'd better get running before you catch your death of cold.

BARDOLPH

(*nods, terrified*)

Thanks, thank you. I will.

AND THEN A SHOT RINGS OUT AND HE CRASHES TO THE GROUND, DEAD. Behind Inman, Sara stands with a rifle.

154. INT. ADA'S BEDROOM, BLACK COVE FARM. MORNING. WINTER 1864.

Ada at the window as, outside, SNOW FLAKES BEGIN TO FALL.

155. EXT. OLD MILL, COLD MOUNTAIN. DAY. WINTER 1864.

THE SNOW HAS STOPPED. It's left a carpet on the ground. Stobrod, Pangle, and Georgia emerge from the Old Mill. THEY MAKE HEAVY FOOTPRINTS as they set off up the hill toward the mountain.

156. EXT. SARA'S CABIN. LATE DAY. WINTER 1864.

THERE'S A HUGE FIRE GOING, WITH A CAULDRON HUNG OVER IT. THE HOG HANGS UPSIDE DOWN FROM A TREE, BLOOD DRIPPING INTO A BOWL. There's a sense of ritual and order as Inman sets about butchering the animal: the chapters of transforming the hog into food.

Sara is inside the cabin, the door open onto the yard. A pot is steaming on the stove. She holds the baby by the fireplace, swaddled up tight. She tries to put him to her breast, but he won't feed. She sings all the while—I dreamed that my bower was full of red swine and my bride bed full of blood—they don't really converse. Inman glances back as he works at the hog, but can hardly bear to, her anxiety so palpable. THE BABY IS DEAD. She looks at it. Kisses its forehead. Makes a strange stifling noise. She puts Ethan back in his crib, comes outside with two plates of food. She serves Inman, gently touching him as she does so. Then serves out food for herself. Inman starts to eat.

SARA

These things are getting wet.

Inman nods. She collects up the knapsacks, including Inman's, and goes back inside the house with them. Inman squats, eating, glancing back toward the cabin. There's the sudden shocking report of a revolver.

Inman, knowing what it is, goes slowly toward the house and its two dead bodies. His own face is a rictus, the eyes thin slits. If he gave into his grief, it would never cease.

157. EXT. THE KILLING GROUND, COLD MOUNTAIN. EVENING. WINTER 1864.

A CLEARING, fringed by poplars. Stobrod is making a fire. Pangle appears with an armful of firewood, his big grin a fixture. Then Georgia appears. He's carrying A SMALL BUCK, frozen and covered with snow.

GEORGIA

What d'you reckon? Think we could eat this?

STOBROD

You cook something long enough, you can eat anything.

PANGLE

(prodding it)
It's froze. How long it been there for?

STOBROD

You hungry?

PANGLE

Yeah.

STOBROD

Not very long.

158. *INT. SARA'S CABIN. DUSK. WINTER 1864.*

From the house, the silhouette of Inman working outside in the day's dying light, snow falling around him. He's digging a grave. Inside the house, TWO BUNDLES, the small body wrapped in a blanket, the other wrapped in the bed's patchwork quilt.

159. EXT. PIGEON RIVER BEHIND THE OLD MILL. DAY. WINTER 1864.

SOME HORSES CLUSTER around the Stobrod party's footprints. Bosie swings acrobatically over his horse to hang over the tracks, then up again into his saddle, looks at Teague. The Home Guard ride forward in the direction of the tracks.

160. EXT. SLOPES OF COLD MOUNTAIN. EVENING. WINTER 1864.

The Home Guard follow the tracks up the mountain.

161. EXT. THE KILLING GROUND, COLD MOUNTAIN. NIGHT. WINTER 1864.

The three men are asleep, lying like petals around the fire. The remains of the deer in evidence.

Suddenly Georgia sits bolt upright, grimaces, gets up and stumbles away from the fire, toward a stand of trees, from which come the vivid sounds of violent nausea.

162. EXT. TREES NEAR THE KILLING GROUND, COLD MOUNTAIN. NIGHT. WINTER 1864.

GEORGIA IS KNEELING, his head in the snow, when he sees HALF A DOZEN RIDERS TROT PAST, approaching the sleeping Stobrod and Pangle. Georgia has to vomit again.

163. EXT. THE KILLING GROUND, COLD MOUNTAIN. NIGHT. WINTER 1864.

Teague rides up to the fire, the other riders with him—Mo, Jo, Bosie, and Grayling. Stobrod wakes, sits up, Pangle sleeps.

> TEAGUE
>
> Evening. Hope we didn't disturb you.

> STOBROD
>
> You're all right.

> TEAGUE
>
> Name's Teague. Do I know you?

> STOBROD
>
> Thewes. Stobrod Thewes.

Teague slides off his horse, approaches the fire.

> TEAGUE
>
> You a deserter?—Don't mind if I just warm up at your fire—
> Stobrod Thewes . . . Stobrod Thewes . . .
> *(of the sleeping Pangle)*
> That your wife?

> STOBROD
>
> Who? That's a he!

> TEAGUE
>
> He your wife?

> STOBROD
>
> We're musicians. He picks the banjo, I got a fiddle.

> TEAGUE
>
> Your sweetheart gots a bit of meat on him.

(to his men)

Look pretty romantic by the fire. Don't they?

BOSIE

It's a picture of love.

164. EXT. TREES NEAR KILLING GROUND, COLD MOUNTAIN.
NIGHT. WINTER 1864.

Georgia squints through the trees. Doesn't know what to do.

165. EXT. THE KILLING GROUND, COLD MOUNTAIN. NIGHT.
WINTER 1864.

Bosie cuts sausage, cooks over the fire.

TEAGUE

Did you answer my question—about your military status?

STOBROD

Discharged. Took a wound at Petersburg.

TEAGUE

Oh, so like a hero's discharge.

STOBROD

I guess.

TEAGUE

And your beloved?

STOBROD

He can't fight. He's simple. He's got a mind no bigger'n a
pickled walnut.

TEAGUE

I'm sorry—he's fat, he's simple and got titties—but you're insisting he ain't a woman. They damn! Don't that sausage smell outstanding.

STOBROD

(he's very nervous)
Mighty outstanding.

TEAGUE

Mighty outstanding! New phrase! Mighty outstanding.

BOSIE

Is he going to play?
(to Stobrod)
You gonna play that fiddle?

STOBROD

Sure. Sure.
(kicks Pangle)
Hey, wake up!

Pangle surfaces, blinks, grins at everybody.

TEAGUE

Evening, Mrs.

PANGLE

(looking around)
Where's Georgia?

TEAGUE

(interested)
Where's Georgia?

In the trees, Georgia ducks, retches.

STOBROD

He don't know what he's saying. We were talking about
Georgia early on—maybe heading down there.

TEAGUE

Georgia's like my armpit. Worse, it's like your armpit.
(to Pangle)
Want some sausage?

PANGLE

Thanks. You is Home Guard?

TEAGUE

Yes, ma'am.

PANGLE

You is Captain Teague?

TEAGUE

I'm known!
(to the others)
I'm known. How am I known?

PANGLE

(quoting)
That bastard Teague.

TEAGUE

Really.

STOBROD

Captain Teague wants us to play.

PANGLE

Love to.

TEAGUE

We heard there were deserters in these parts. Hiding out in a big cave.

STOBROD

Not come to my ears.

TEAGUE

You don't know where this cave is?

STOBROD

No, sir.

PANGLE

You do, Stobes! He means—

STOBROD

Right, right! No, there is a cave, right, up near Bearpen Branch. We played some music up there, never occurred to me they were outliers.

PANGLE

Ain't nowhere near Bearpen Branch! He's always getting lost. That cave—we live there!—it's east toward Big Stomp. Tell you how I always find it. You go round and round in a circle, except you're going up, and then there's a big old locust tree fell down across the path, points straight at it, like a finger. You gets to the tree, sit on it, and there's your entrance, tree points straight at it. Except I don't sit on it no more, on account of the twigs tearing at my new coat. I like my coat.

TEAGUE

It's a good coat.

PANGLE

Ruby made me up this coat. This part belonged to a reverend, this part belonged to a horse. Ruby says—what is it—I should pray or neigh, depending.

TEAGUE
(*impassive, but registering these involuntary betrayals*)
Sounds good. Let's eat, let's hear some mighty outstanding music.

166. EXT. TREES NEAR KILLING GROUND, COLD MOUNTAIN. NIGHT. WINTER 1864.

Georgia watches as the music starts, Stobrod playing and singing, Pangle joining in at the chorus. THEN TEAGUE DECIDES TO SING A VERSE, WITH GREAT SINCERITY.

167. EXT. THE KILLING GROUND, COLD MOUNTAIN. NIGHT. WINTER 1864.

Something like compassion has flickered over Teague's face. Mo and Jo nod to the music's secret rhythms. Only Bosie seems detached, contemplating his long fingernail. The music finishes.

PANGLE
What d'you make of that?

BOSIE
(*getting up, impatient*)
Broke my young heart.

STOBROD
(*knowing what is to come and desperate about Ruby and Ada*)
Ruby, she don't know one end of the war from the other. Don't you worry yourself about her, is what I'm saying. Or Ada.

TEAGUE

(indicating an upturned tree, its root like a huge fan)
Stand over there.

STOBROD

Do you know what I'm saying?

TEAGUE

You heard me. And him.

Stobrod gets up, carrying his fiddle, nods at Pangle.

STOBROD

Come on.

Pangle gets up, banjo in his hand. Puts his arm around Stobrod as if they
were about to be photographed. The Home Guard gather around them.
From the trees Georgia watches, helpless. Pangle grins at Teague.

TEAGUE

Don't smile.

PANGLE

What?

TEAGUE

Quit smiling.

STOBROD

He always smiles. He don't mean nothing by it. I told him
this world's got nothing worth a smile.

TEAGUE

Put your hat over your face.

PANGLE

What do you mean?

Cover your face with your hat.

Pangle takes off his hat, holds it over his face. The moment he obliges, Teague walks over and shoots him through the hat. Stobrod makes to run, but Bosie has produced his pistol and shoots. Stobrod collapses in the snow.

168. EXT. TREES NEAR THE KILLING GROUND, COLD MOUNTAIN. NIGHT. WINTER 1864.

Georgia lies prostrate in the snow, shuddering under the report of each bullet.

169. EXT. LAST LIGHT. WINTER 1864.

The snow falls down on Inman. He's hardly visible in its gusting waves. Just a thin black question mark, hunched over the elements, moving slowly forward . . .

170. EXT. PATH IN THE MOUNTAINS. DAY. WINTER 1864.

Inman comes sliding down a crumbling slate hill and onto the path. He comes to a place where the path suddenly drops away to reveal a view of the geography. And there, finally, in the distance, Inman can see the Blue Ridge Mountains. Somewhere in there is home, is Ada. He goes on.

171. EXT. BOTTOM FIELD, BLACK COVE FARM. DAY. WINTER 1864.

Ruby working in the snow, in the field, clipping a sheep's feet, the animal on its back between Ruby's knees.

She looks up to see GEORGIA RUNNING ACROSS THE FIELD TOWARDS HER, calling out her name.

GEORGIA

Ruby! They shot Pangle . . . and they shot Stobrod.

From the kitchen window, Ada looks on as he reaches Ruby, the story pouring from him. Ada emerges from the house, walks towards the bad news.

172. INT. STOREROOM, BLACK COVE FARM. DAY.
WINTER 1864.

Ruby sorting out a kit of shovels, blankets. Ada comes in, doesn't know how to help her friend, who shows no emotion.

ADA

I told Georgia he can stop here, sleep in the barn. He's got nothing inside him. He'd walk out of here and die in the snow.

RUBY

He can milk the cows. I was worrying about that. It'll be dark in a couple of hours. It's ten hours climb from here. He's drawn a map.

ADA

I'm ready.

RUBY

(boiling)
You know those fools stayed the night in the Mill? That's Stobrod Thewes—he can't do one good thing without adding the bad. Left tracks in the snow all the way up for them Home Guards to follow. That's a sign says shoot me!

Ruby, I'm so sorry.

Ada moves toward her, puts her arms around her. Ruby is rigid. Ada stops
embracing her.

RUBY

We should get going.

Ruby's tying up the kit. She doesn't know how to grieve.

RUBY (CONT.)

Every piece of this is man's bullshit. They call this war a cloud
over the land, but they made the weather. Then they stand in
the rain and say: shit! it's raining!
(tears welling)
If I cry one tear for my daddy, I stole it off a crocodile.

173. EXT. COLD MOUNTAIN. EVENING. WINTER 1864.

THE SNOW IS FALLING HEAVILY. RUBY AND ADA TRUDGE UP
THE MOUNTAIN, dressed in Monroe's clothes, hats pulled down, lead-
ing the horse, which is loaded up with tools and supplies. A choice of
paths. They start up one, then Ruby decides against it, consults the map,
and they reverse, pulling the horse back and then yanking it up the other
path.

174. EXT. STRUCTURE, COLD MOUNTAIN. NIGHT.
WINTER 1864.

Ruby and Ada have made a fire. They sleep under a stone structure, which forms a
natural Π *shape, the fire in the entrance, the snow caught in its light.*

175. EXT. CHAPEL, COLD MOUNTAIN. EARLY MORNING. WINTER 1864.

Cold Mountain Town dipped in snow, the street empty. A dog. Inman appears from behind a building, wary, and approaches the chapel. Inman wipes the snow from the cluster of votives on the chapel. He sees the names of so many he knew, their faces.

176. EXT. BLACK COVE. WINTER GARDEN. MORNING. WINTER 1864.

Inman arrives at the edge of Black Cove Farm. HE SEES ADA STANDING IN THE FIELD, arms partly outstretched toward him. He quickens, only to understand that he's looking at a scarecrow. He approaches it, sees it's wearing the outfit he last saw Ada in. He touches the materials, now just ominous tatters.

177. EXT. BLACK COVE FARM. MORNING. WINTER 1864.

Georgia hurries from the barn toward the privy, the snow scarred with evidence of his many trips back and forth. Inman steps out, his pistol flashing in his hand.

> INMAN
> *You stop right where you're stood.*

> GEORGIA
> *Mister, shoot me, or let me get to the privy—I don't care which.*

> INMAN
> *Where's the Reverend Monroe?*

Georgia shakes his head and is inside the privy in a second.

> GEORGIA (OFF)
> *Don't know a Monroe. They're two females here, run the place. One's got the name of Ruby. She's Stobrod's girl. He's the fiddle player.*

INMAN

And the other woman?
(realizes he can't easily describe Ada)
—got her hair wound up all particular in back, not a Highland
woman, a woman who stands out, anyway . . .

GEORGIA (OFF)

Ada.

INMAN

That's right. Her name's Ada.

GEORGIA (OFF)

They're up in the mountain. Home Guard caught up with three of us
outliers, shot the other two dead on the ground. Right up Cold
Mountain. I got the screamers, otherwise I'd be lying dead next to them.
Girls went up with shovels to bury them.

Inman is swaying a little, exhaustion, anticlimax catching up with him. Through
a crack in the privy, Georgia catches sight of Inman sitting down in the snow, run-
ning a hand over his face in a secret and terrible weariness. He comes out.

GEORGIA (cont.)

You could go inside the house, there's a fire. Better than the snow.

INMAN

Just draw me a map and I'll be moving on.

GEORGIA

It's a long walk.

INMAN

I've been on a long walk.

178. EXT. THE KILLING GROUND, COLD MOUNTAIN.
MORNING. WINTER 1864.

Ada and Ruby arrive at the scene of murder. Pangle is keeled over in the bole of the fallen tree, snow covering him. Ada brushes some of the snow from his face, revealing the death wound, then lays a hand in blessing on his head.

RUBY

(behind her, of Stobrod)
He ain't here.

ADA

I don't understand.

RUBY

Maybe Teague's took him. They did that with the Swanger boys—didn't they? Strung them up as warning . . .

ADA

They took his coat. Why would they take his coat?

Ada fishes out Pangle's banjo from the snow. It's broken and the strings hang slack.

RUBY HAS WANDERED OVER TO THE EDGE OF THE CLEAR-ING, LOOKS DOWN TO SEE STOBROD LYING AT THE BOT-TOM OF THE SLOPE, blood everywhere, staining the crust of snow that covers him.

RUBY

Daddy! Daddy!

Ruby hurtles to her father, all her love contained in the urgency with which she slides down the bank. She puts a head to his chest, seeks out a pulse at his wrist. Calls back to Ada.

RUBY (CONT.)

He's still breathing!
(to Stobrod)

They damn! Daddy, Daddy—it's Ruby. Don't you die on me
again.

(to Ada)

He's still breathing!

179. EXT. THE KILLING GROUND, COLD MOUNTAIN.
AFTERNOON. WINTER 1864.

A mean fire burns by the creek. RUBY TURNS A KNIFE IN THE
FLAMES. Ada loads a pan with snow to boil over the fire. Stobrod's back
is exposed. Just by the shoulder blade is an ugly gray and purple bulge
the size of a crab apple. Ruby cuts the skin and prizes out a ball. Stobrod
doesn't move.

                    ADA

Let's get him home. We have herbs there and it's warm.

                    RUBY

He'll die first. He's got hardly no blood left in him.

                    ADA

He'll die lying here.

180. EXT. BY THE OUTLIERS' CAVE, COLD MOUNTAIN. AFTER-
NOON. WINTER 1864.

Teague sits on the trunk of a fallen tree, looking straight ahead to where the mouth
of a cave winks back at him. He runs his hand along the trunk until it snags on a
twig. Beside him, Bosie loads his pistol.

181. EXT. CHEROKEE VILLAGE. COLD MOUNTAIN. AFTER-
NOON. WINTER 1864.

There's a stream and, up on the bank, A CLUSTER OF BLACK CONI-CAL HUTS, made up of chestnut logs, abandoned and slightly sinister looking.

> RUBY (V.O.)
> There's a place further on up. Used to be. Old Cherokee place.
> Got shelter and good water.

Ada and Ruby approach one of the huts, its door long lost. The snow has drifted in. A second hut has a door, which they pry open. It's dark and cold, but apparently still weatherproof. They get Stobrod off the horse and carry him inside, then come out again to unload the horse of its remaining load.

> ADA
> *This horse is weary. He's ready to give up the ghost.*

Ruby picks up the blankets and provisions and goes back inside to her father. Ada takes the horse to another hut and, despite his great reluctance, pushes him inside.

> ADA *(cont.)*
> Good boy.
> (*she blows into his nostrils, calming him*)
> That's warmer, isn't it.

Ada wouldn't even recognize this practical, hardy woman she's become. Stringy and of few words. She sets off toward the tree tunnel, passing Stobrod's hut.

> ADA (CONT.)
> I'm getting firewood.

182. EXT. THE KILLING GROUND, COLD MOUNTAIN. DUSK.
WINTER 1864.

Inman approaches the Killing Ground. He studies the ground, finds Pangle's grave. Then his curiosity changes to urgency. Blood has left its black writing in the snow and he finds the journey away, still tiny telltale spatters of blood, and the hoof and boot prints of two walkers and one loaded horse. Inman follows the tracks, knowing he's looking for Ada.

183. INT. STOBROD'S HUT, CHEROKEE VILLAGE. NIGHT. WINTER 1864.

The fire burns, a pall of smoke. Stobrod lies on the ground, swathed in blankets. Coughs. Ruby sits next to him, wipes the hair from his forehead. Ada opens her eyes, looks, closes them, listens to the fire, a strange squeaking as it burns.

> ADA
>
> That wood—that sound when it burns—that mean more snow?

> RUBY
>
> Yes, it do, country girl.

184. EXT. TRACK, COLD MOUNTAIN. DAWN. WINTER 1864.

First light. The sun creeps up, a red streak of dawn. Inman walking, his head bent to the tracks. He walks quickly, even as the terrain grows more steep. As he bends to the snow—where a spot of blood has fallen into a hoofprint—A FLAKE OF SNOW LANDS ON HIS HAND. Then a second. He looks up. The snow falls. He starts to move more quickly, racing the snow.

185. EXT. BLACK COVE FARM. DAWN. WINTER 1864.

Georgia emerges, hurries to the privy. Once inside, he's yanking off his britches with some urgency, when THE DOOR EXPLODES! A shotgun has blasted a huge hole, its beads cutting Georgia. The hole reveals Teague, standing in the snow, gun raised.

> TEAGUE
>
> When you're ready . . .

Behind him, his guard, and their trophies from the cave: A LITTER OF CORPSES, HALF A DOZEN MEN ROPED TO THE BACK OF GRAYLING'S HORSE. Georgia comes out of the privy, bleeding from a hundred tiny cuts.

186. EXT. THREE-WAY CROSSING, COLD MOUNTAIN. MORNING. WINTER 1864.

The snow falls more heavily. Inman hurries, head down, pursuing the tracks. As he approaches a crossroads, the tracks become fainter and fainter, then disappear. He's at a loss.

187. EXT. GORGE NEAR CHEROKEE VILLAGE. MORNING. WINTER 1864.

In the cleft of the gorge, A DOZEN WILD TURKEYS pick their way across the snow. A shotgun lines up its sight at one of them. The trigger is squeezed. An explosion of feathers.

188. EXT. GORGE BELOW CHEROKEE VILLAGE. MORNING. WINTER 1864.

Ada collects the turkey, the first creature she's ever shot. Doesn't quite know how to hold it. She straightens up and sees, at the other end of the gorge, backlit by the morning sun, THE SILHOUETTE OF A MAN. She drops the turkey, tries to reload the shotgun.

ADA
Turn round and go back where you came from.

Inman is bewildered by this woman's voice in a man's outfit, keeps walking, peering through the snow. Ada fires a warning shot. Inman, still some distance, suddenly understands.

> INMAN

Ada? Ada Monroe?

Ada, unprepared, thrown, doesn't respond. After all this time, all this way, Inman could give up the ghost.

> INMAN (CONT.)

I believe I made a mistake.

He turns, walks heavily away from her. Then he turns again, completely lost, without compass.

> INMAN *(cont.)*

If I knew where to go, I'd go there.

> ADA

Inman.

He nods. They don't know how to speak to each other, just stand awkwardly, some distance apart, the emotion stones in their throats. Eventually—

> ADA (CONT.)

You'd better come with me.

189. INT. STOBROD'S HUT, CHEROKEE VILLAGE. MORNING. WINTER 1864.

Ada enters, Inman behind her. Ruby looks up from Stobrod.

> ADA

Ruby, this is Inman.

Ruby digests this. Considers this ghost of a man.

RUBY

Congratulations, I should send you out with a shotgun more often. He looks as if he could topple over.

INMAN

I may need to.

RUBY

Be my guest. You shot or something?

INMAN

Not lately.

RUBY

Hungry?
(Inman nods, Ruby to Ada)
He woke up.

ADA

Stobrod?

RUBY

Said—"your mommy's name was Grace"—then closed his eyes again.

190. EXT. CHEROKEE VILLAGE. DAY. WINTER 1864.

Ada comes out of Stobrod's hut, a glimpse of Inman sleeping on the floor, heads for another hut that Ruby is sweeping out. The snow has stopped. Ada stands in the door, watching Ruby. Ruby's resistance to Inman is palpable.

ADA

He's asleep. They both are.

RUBY

I'm not surprised. Your man looks tuckered out.

ADA

I saw him. In Sally Swanger's well. A man like a black smudge in the snow, the sun behind him.

RUBY

Well, there you are.

ADA

But it wasn't the same. What I saw. It wasn't snowing. And in the well, he was, as if he were falling.

RUBY

You probably don't remember it right.

ADA

I remember it exactly. There were crows, these black crows flying towards me. I thought I was seeing him fall. Instead I was seeing him come back to me. All this while I've been packing ice around my heart. How will I make it melt?

RUBY

Better get a fire going.
(goes to the fireplace)
I've got big plans for that farm. Got a vision in my mind of how that Cove needs to be.

ADA

I know you have.

RUBY

There's not a thing we can't do ourselves.

191. EXT. CHEROKEE VILLAGE. DAY. WINTER 1864.

Inman is washing and attempting to hack off his beard with Ruby's knife. Behind him Ada is at a fire working at plucking the turkey. Ruby approaches him.

> RUBY
>
> You finishing with my knife?

> INMAN
>
> Just about.

> RUBY
>
> We got a bird to cook.
> (*of his shaving*)
> You're making a pig's ear of that job. Give it to me.

Ruby takes the knife and begins to shave him herself.

> RUBY (CONT.)
>
> I won't cut you. But if I do, I can't see it'll make much difference. You got the right feelings for her?

Inman nods.

> RUBY (CONT.)
>
> Don't move your head.

> INMAN
>
> I do.

192. INT. ADA AND RUBY HUT, CHEROKEE VILLAGE. NIGHT. WINTER 1864.

THE FIRE BURNS. Ada lies awake. Ruby sleeping. Ada gets up, steps out into the snow, her blanket around her.

193. EXT. ADA AND RUBY'S HUT, CHEROKEE VILLAGE. NIGHT. WINTER 1864.

Inman is outside his hut. Only the light escaping from the hut fire lights them; they're almost silhouettes.

> INMAN
>
> I'm sorry. I was trying to be quiet.

> ADA
>
> I couldn't sleep.

> INMAN
>
> —I got no appetite left to be in a room with wounded men.

> ADA
>
> I can't see your face.

> INMAN
>
> It's not a face you recognized.

> ADA
>
> Did you get my letters?

> INMAN
>
> I got three letters. Carried them in that book you gave me. The Bartram.

> ADA
>
> I probably sent a hundred and three. Did you write to me?

> INMAN
>
> Whenever I could. If you never got them, I can summarize.

> ADA
>
> No, it's—

INMAN

I pray you're well. I pray I'm in your thoughts. You are all that keeps me from sliding into some dark place.

ADA

But how did I keep you? We barely knew each other. A few moments.

INMAN

A thousand moments. They're like a bag of tiny diamonds glittering in a black heart. Don't matter if they're real or things I made up. The shape of your neck. The way you felt under my hands when I pulled you to me.

ADA

You're plowing a field.

INMAN

You're carrying a tray.

ADA

I'm playing a piano and you're standing outside. You wouldn't come in. That's why I had to carry a tray.

INMAN

That kiss—which I've kissed every day of my walking.

ADA

Every day of my waiting.

INMAN

Maybe you can't see my face, but if you could see my inside, my whatever you want to name it, my spirit, that's the fear I have deeper than any gash on my neck. I think I'm ruined. They kept trying to put me in the ground, but I wasn't ready, no ma'am, no more ready than that scoundrel in there's not ready to die on us. But if I had goodness, I lost it. If I had anything tender in me, I shot it dead.

Ruby stomps out of the hut.

RUBY

Number one—shut this door, it's freezing.
(*goes over to Stobrod's hut*)
Number two—shut that door, it's freezing.
(*turns to them*)
I'm laying on my back, with my fingers poked in my ears trying to shut out who's got a bag of diamonds and who's carrying a tray. If you want to get three feet up a bull's ass, listen to what sweethearts whisper to each other.

She's at the door to Stobrod's hut. She contemplates them.

RUBY (CONT.)

In fact, if you're going to wimble all night, I'm going to sleep in with him.

And with that, she enters Stobrod's hut, slamming the door.

ADA

Now I can't see anything.

A long pause.

INMAN

I'll say good night.

ADA

No. Don't.

194. INT. ADA AND RUBY'S HUT, CHEROKEE VILLAGE. NIGHT. WINTER 1864.

Ada puts logs onto the fire. After a few moments, a knock.

ADA

Come in.

Inman enters. They don't know the rules for this.

ADA (CONT.)

Whatever comes to pass between you and me, I want Ruby to stay in Black Cove.

INMAN

Right.

ADA

As long as she wants. And if she never leaves, I'll be glad.

INMAN

More a question could she put up with me.

ADA

And you understand she's my friend, she's not a hired hand and she doesn't empty a night jar unless it's her own.

INMAN

Fair enough.

ADA

This war's made some things pointless. It's hard to imagine a wedding. I think even my father would recognize that.

INMAN

Ada, I want to marry you. If you'll have me.

ADA

Isn't there some religion where you just have to say I marry you, three times, and then you're man and wife?

INMAN

I marry you, I marry you, I marry you.

Ada laughs, unsettling Inman.

INMAN (CONT.)

Why's that funny?

ADA

No, I think it's I divorce you three times, and then you're not married anymore.

INMAN

I can wait for you.

ADA

You waited enough. I certainly did.
I marry you. I marry you. I marry you.

And they kiss, tentative, then more urgent.

ADA (CONT.)

I'm sorry about the way I look. In these clothes.
(Inman shakes his head)
And there are so many buttons.
(starts to undress)
Will you turn your back?

INMAN

No. No, I won't.

And he watches as she begins to undo the rosary of buttons. Their nervous hands helping each other.

195. INT. ADA'S BEDROOM, BLACK COVE FARM. NIGHT. WINTER 1864.

Teague sits at Ada's dressing table. He picks up her hairbrush, teases out a long hair from its bristles, which he considers, then begins to brush his own hair. Bosie appears.

BOSIE
So where are they?

TEAGUE
I think tonight, Daddy Bear's going to sleep in Goldilocks's bed.

He goes to Ada's bed, tugs off his boots, and slides, fully dressed, under the covers.

196. INT. ADA AND RUBY'S HUT, CHEROKEE VILLAGE. NIGHT. WINTER 1864

Firelight shadows. Ada and Inman making love. So delicate.

Later: Embers. Ada washing Inman, flannel to his back. He starts to sob. The wait, the yearning, unraveling. Ada comforts him. And they fold into another embrace.

197. EXT. CHEROKEE VILLAGE. MORNING. WINTER 1864.

A crisp, cold, beautiful morning. Inman prepares the horse. Ada is bringing bundles. As Ruby emerges from Stobrod's hut, she sees them, for the first time, laughing. She approaches.

INMAN
You go ahead. I'll follow with the horse at a pace your daddy can tolerate.

ADA

We can all go together.

INMAN

It's safer this way. No one has quarrel with you.

RUBY

He's right.

INMAN

(to Ruby)
I gather I need permission from you, Ruby, if I reckon on living at Black Cove.

Ruby gives a curt nod, goes over to Stobrod's hut. Inman gets close to Ada.

ADA

I don't want to let you go.

INMAN

We'll get to you by nightfall.

ADA

You be safe.

She puts her hand to his mouth, which creases into a smile.

198. INT. STOBROD'S HUT, CHEROKEE VILLAGE. DAY.
WINTER 1864.

Ruby is wrapping a fragile Stobrod for the journey. He's still not fully coherent, but agitated, delirious.

STOBROD

> Be careful . . . Teague . . .
> (Ruby nods)
> Careful.
> (he coughs)
> He's sweet on you, that Georgia boy.

He coughs for a long time. Ruby's tender.

RUBY

> If you say a thing and then cough it's a lie. Daddy, stay on that horse,
> and don't lose him or sell him. We'll need him on the farm.

199. EXT. CHEROKEE VILLAGE. MORNING. WINTER 1864.

The two women are tramping away in the snow. Inman watches, *then turns
towards Stobrod's hut. He opens the door. Stobrod looks up at him.*

STOBROD

> I know you, don't I? From the war.

INMAN

> Yes, you do.

STOBROD

> We're survivors.

200. EXT. TRACK, COLD MOUNTAIN. DAY. WINTER 1864.

Ruby and Ada walk.

RUBY

I hope that Georgia boy's been seeing to the animals.

ADA

I thought you were thinking on him!

RUBY

I was not. I was thinking on swollen udders—and before you say same difference . . . !

ADA

I'm saying nothing.

Ruby elbows her.

RUBY

Miss lovey-dovey!

Ada elbows her back. A sudden voice freezes her blood.

TEAGUE (V.O.)

That was a long funeral for your daddy!

Emerging from the trees, coming up the path, TIED TO THE BACK OF THE LITTER IS A BRUISED AND BLOODY GEORGIA. TEAGUE HAS PANGLE'S COAT WARMING HIS KNEES.

BOSIE

That was a wake!

TEAGUE

That was Irish! Your friend Georgia, here—we went down to visit you—after we heard you were harboring deserters—and he told us you were up here.

BOSIE

We're up and down this mountain!

ADA

There'll be a reckoning. The war is over. And then there'll be a reckoning.

TEAGUE

(to Ruby)

You make this coat? I know it's half horse, half reverend. Been keeping my vitals warm as a woman's—I nearly said a bad word.

RUBY

I should thank you.

TEAGUE

You're welcome. What did I do?

RUBY

Clarified my way of thinking. About love. I love my daddy. About hate.

TEAGUE

Funny, your daddy was turning his friend into a woman, you turning yours into a man. Biology, what's happened to it?
(turns on Ada)
Reckoning? The reckoning is for your world, not mine.

And then, all of a sudden, STOBROD, TIED TO THE HORSE, COMES INTO VIEW, RIDING STRAIGHT AT THE GROUP, DISTURBING THEM. Teague can't credit it.

TEAGUE (CONT.)

They damn! That's a hard bastard to kill.

As he reaches for his carbine, Ruby raises her shotgun and shoots him, catching him in the shoulder, great damage. He stays on his horse. Bosie immediately shoots Ruby, who drops to the ground, wounded. Then Inman, coming from the trees, is among them, firing the Colt revolver, killing first Mo, then—as Stobrod rides his horse against his—Jo. Then Inman is pursuing Grayling, firing, pulling down the horse. As the odds diminish, Bosie decides to make a getaway, riding back up the path. Ruby sits up. Teague is recovering, pulling out his gun, looking for Inman. Ada runs toward Mo's discarded saber and, tackling horse and rider, manages to run Teague through, pulling him off his horse. Inman kills Grayling and comes back toward Ada, who stands over Teague, the blood blotting the snow under him. Teague looks at her, sad.

Inman picks up the Spencer carbine, turns to look where Bosie has gone, steps up onto Teague's horse, reins the horse in, LEANS OVER, AND SHOOTS TEAGUE DEAD. He turns the horse in the direction Bosie had headed. He can't see horse or rider, but in the stand of hickory trees ahead, THE GUSTS OF STEAMING BREATH betray them both. He rides slowly toward the stand of trees. Behind him, Ada runs to Ruby, tends to her.

201. EXT. GORGE, COLD MOUNTAIN. DAY. WINTER 1864.

Bosie gallops through the gorge, heading back up the mountain. Inman chases, some distance behind.

202. EXT. STAND OF TREES, COLD MOUNTAIN. DAY. WINTER 1864.

Inman arrives at a stand of beech trees. Bosie is there, horse and rider exposed from the cover of trees by steaming gusts of breath. Inman's horse is parallel to Bosie, who is deep inside the trees but also riding, slowly. It's like a dance.

INMAN

Come down from there . . .

BOSIE

No, sir. Here's fine.

INMAN

I just have to shoot the horse from under you.

BOSIE

Shoot her. She's not mine. You riding Captain Teague's mare?

INMAN

I am.

BOSIE

He dead?

INMAN

I hope so.

Bosie's nose starts to bleed. He tilts his head back. Inman is suddenly so weary.

INMAN (CONT.)

Look, give me your gun and ride home. I'm done fighting. I'm sick of it.

BOSIE

I give you my gun, you'll shoot me dead.

INMAN

I will not shoot you, but nor am I walking down that mountain looking over my shoulder for you.

BOSIE

That's what they call a conundrum. I tell you what I've got on my side.

INMAN

What have you got on your side?

The confidence of youth.

And in that second HE PRODUCES HIS GUN AND FIRES. INMAN HAS ALREADY FIRED AND THE BOY, SHOT IN THE HEAD, FALLS, CAUGHT BY ONE STIRRUP, THE HORSE BOLTING. INMAN WATCHES, STOCK-STILL, THEN MAKES A COUGH, AS IF CLEARING HIS THROAT, AND A THIN MIST OF BLOOD SPRAYS FROM HIS MOUTH.

203. EXT. RIDGE, COLD MOUNTAIN. DAY. WINTER 1864.

Ada has untied Georgia, who hurries to Ruby. Then, at the sound of the shots, Ada starts to run up the path, collecting a shotgun.

204. EXT. A GORGE, COLD MOUNTAIN. DAY. WINTER 1864.

THE GROUND SIMPLIFIES AND ADA IS AT THE BOTTOM OF THE GORGE. A STEEP INCLINE, THE SUN LOW AND IN FRONT OF HER. SHE SEES A FUNNEL OF ROCKS, AND THEN A SUD-DEN FLURRY OF ANGRY CROWS FLYING TOWARDS HER. AT THE TOP OF THE GORGE IS A SMALL HIEROGLYPH OF A MAN. FINALLY, THE IMAGE FROM THE SWANGER WELL EXACTLY AS SHE FIRST SAW IT. THE FIGURE RAISES A HAND, BRIEFLY, THEN PITCHES FORWARD INTO THE SNOW.

She runs, her heart broken, toward the body of Inman. He's dying, the red flag of his life ebbing away in the snow. Ada falls to her knees and pulls him over, the snow crusted on his face, which she wipes away with great tenderness. She sits, his head in her lap, and watches over him as he looks at her for a moment and then closes his eyes.

A VIOLIN PLAYS, quite raucous.

205. INT. KITCHEN, BLACK COVE FARM. DAY. EASTER 1871.

A GIRL, about five or six, with Ada's curls, sits at the table cradling a tiny lamb, which won't feed from the nippled bottle she offers it. She tries again. Ada comes in suddenly, takes a knife from the kitchen, and hurries out.

>   ADA
> You bring that lamb outside.

The girl gets up and carries the lamb out into the field.

206. EXT. TOP FIELD, BLACK COVE FARM. DAY. EASTER 1871.

THE SOUND OF THE FIDDLE CONTINUING, JOINED BY A BANJO. A glorious spring morning, Black Cove Farm at its most luxuriant, the path edged with brilliant flowers. There are more animals in evidence. The girl emerges from the house and sees Ada in the field, surrounded by sheep. She hurries over. ADA IS EXPERTLY SKINNING A STILLBORN LAMB. The little girl, Ada's daughter, is horrified.

>   GRACE
> What are you doing?

>   ADA
> He died in the night, love.

She has the skin off the lamb, which lies like a little pink cat on the ground. She approaches Grace, takes the live lamb from her arms; the girl is resistant, frightened.

>   GRACE
> Don't kill him!

>   ADA
> I'm not going to kill him. But we have to try something or else he's going to die.

She takes the skin and wraps it around Grace's lamb. Then she puts the covered lamb into the pen with the dead lamb's mother. It goes to the sheep and, after a few false starts, starts to feed, accepted as a surrogate.

> ADA (CONT.)
>
> Isn't that a small mercy.

And A VOICE joins in with the fiddle and banjo.

> ADA (V.O.)
>
> There are days now, when I manage not to think of you—when the needs of our daughter or the farm call with more urgency than my heart. This time of year, there's so much life everywhere. I find you in all of it as though you were still walking back to me, or because I know I am slowly walking home to you.

207. EXT. BLACK COVE FARM. DAY. EASTER 1871.

STOBROD is playing, on his repaired fiddle. His hair is now completely gray. GEORGIA is playing the banjo and singing, although A SMALL CHILD keeps invading his picking hand trying to join in. RUBY HAS ANOTHER GEORGIA CHILD IN HER ARMS, but is also trying to serve food. She passes Georgia and touches the top of his head. SALLY SWANGER is pouring water from a jug. Ada emerges from the kitchen with a big pie, racing to the table, laughing at the heat of it.

> ADA
>
> Hot hot hot hot hot!!!

From behind her, Grace appears, carrying a jug of milk, puts it on the groaning board of the table. Grace has a full plate in front of her, and picks up a fork to spear some meat.

> ADA (CONT'D)
>
> Grace Inman, nobody said eat.

(then to Stobrod)
Mr. Thewes . . .

The music stops. And there's quiet except for the sound of animals: low-ing, barking, braying, bleating.

ADA (CONT.)
For good friends, good food, good family: for all our blessings
—oh Lord, we thank thee. Amen.

ALL
Amen!

And they eat.

ADA (V.O.)
I looked once more down Sally Swanger's well, and this time there was nothing there to haunt me—just clouds, clouds and then sun.

THE END